Illustrated Children's Bible

Retold by James F. Couch, Jr.
Illustrated by Geoffrey Brittingham

Ideals Children's Books • Nashville, Tennessee
an imprint of Hambleton-Hill Publishing, Inc.

Published by Ideals Children's Books
An imprint of Hambleton-Hill Publishing, Inc.
Nashville, Tennessee 37218

Printed and bound in the United States of America

Library of Congress Cataloging-in-Publication Data

Couch, James F.
   Illustrated children's Bible / retold by James F. Couch, Jr. : illustrated by Geoffrey Brittingham.
       p.   cm.
   ISBN 1-57102-018-7
   1. Bible—Paraphrases, English. 2. Bible—Illustrations.
I. Brittingham, Geoffrey. II. Title.
BS551.2.C69 1995
220.9'505—dc20   94-32772
                                                              CIP
                                                              AC

Contents

The Old Testament

Contents

The New Testament

GENESIS 1; 2:1–3
Creation

In the beginning there was no earth, no sky, and no universe. But there was always God.

Then God created heaven and earth. He made the sun, the moon, the stars, and the sky. God gathered the waters from the land and formed seas, rivers, and streams. Then he filled the land with trees and plants. Next God made creatures of all sorts and sizes to live on the earth and in the sea and to soar through the sky.

God saw that all he had made was good. But there was still no one to help care for the earth and its creatures. There was no one to love God and to talk to him. So God made man and woman in his own likeness. God blessed them and said, "Have many children to live on the earth and to rule over it wisely."

The work of creation had taken six days. On the seventh day, God rested.

5

In the Garden of Eden

God planted a beautiful garden in the east. He called it the Garden of Eden, and there he put Adam, the first man.

God planted two special trees in the garden, the Tree of Life and the Tree of the Knowledge of Good and Evil. God told Adam he could eat the fruit of any tree except the Tree of the Knowledge of Good and Evil. "If you eat from that tree, you will die," said God.

So Adam lived in the garden and cared for it. God brought every living creature to Adam, and Adam gave them names. But God could see that Adam was lonely, so he made a companion for Adam, a woman. Adam named her Eve, and they were very happy together.

But one day a wicked serpent came up to Eve and whispered, "If you eat from the Tree of the Knowledge of Good and Evil, you won't really die. You will become as wise as God."

Eve wanted to be as wise as God. She looked around her. Then she stretched out her hand, picked a fruit, and ate it. It was delicious.

"Adam!" she called. "Try this fruit!"

And he did.

Immediately the happy peacefulness of the garden was destroyed. Adam and Eve became anxious because they were naked, and they hurried to cover themselves with fig leaves.

By then it was evening, and God was walking in the garden in the cool of the day. Feeling afraid and guilty, Adam and Eve hid among the trees. But God knew what they had done.

"Have you eaten from the forbidden tree?" God asked.

Adam tried to escape blame. "The woman told me to," he said.

God looked at Eve and asked, "Why did you do it?"

"The serpent made me!" cried Eve.

God was very angry. He commanded that the serpent would have to crawl on the ground from that moment on and that people would always be its enemy. To Eve, God said, "From now on, when women have children, they will suffer pain." And to Adam, he said, "For as long as men live, they will always have to work hard to get a harvest from the earth."

Then God made clothes for them from the skins of animals and sent them out of the garden. Adam and Eve could never return. God placed an angel and a flaming sword to guard the way to the Tree of Life. Because Adam and Eve had eaten the forbidden fruit, they would grow old and one day die.

GENESIS 4:1–26

Two Brothers

Life outside the garden was very different for Adam and Eve. They had to work hard, but God still loved and cared for them. Eventually Eve had two sons, Cain and Abel. As the boys grew up, they helped with the work. Cain became a farmer and Abel became a shepherd.

In those days, offerings were made to God to show love for him and to thank God for his love and care. One day Cain and Abel made an offering to the Lord. Cain brought some of the harvest from his fields. But he didn't bring it out of love and thanks. He didn't want to make the offering at all.

Abel brought the best from his freshly killed sheep, and he gladly offered it to God.

God accepted Abel's gift, but he refused Cain's.

8

Cain was furiously jealous of his brother. Pretending to be friendly, Cain asked Abel to come with him into the fields. But once they were alone, Cain suddenly hit Abel and killed him.

Thinking no one would find out, Cain left his brother's body where it lay and came home as if nothing had happened.

But God knew what Cain had done, and he cursed Cain, saying, "Never again will you get a harvest from the ground. You will leave here and wander the earth for the rest of your life."

God then put a mark on Cain so that no one would harm him, but everyone would know he had killed his brother.

Cain left his home and moved toward the east. Adam and Eve had another son, Seth. In his turn, Seth married and had children. And their children had children, and so on, until there were many people living on the earth.

Noah

God looked at the world he had made and the people he had made. He saw people killing one another, robbing, cheating, and quarreling with one another. And God became sorry he had made them.

Only one man was different—Noah. Noah still loved God and God loved him.

One day God spoke to Noah. "I am going to destroy these people because of the way they are behaving. I am going to send a great flood over the earth. All life under the skies will be destroyed."

Noah was afraid, but God said, "Do not fear. You are a good man. I will not destroy you or your family."

Then God told Noah to build an Ark. He told him what materials to use and how big to make the Ark. Then God said, "You must bring into the Ark pairs of all the creatures that live, one male and one female for each pair. And you must take all the different kinds of food that will be needed and store the food in the Ark."

The task was enormous! But Noah trusted God, so he and his family set to work hammering, sawing, and shaping the wood. The people who lived nearby laughed and jeered at them.

But Noah went on building. At last the Ark was finished. Leaves, hay, fruit, and grains were gathered and stored inside the Ark. Just as Noah was wondering how he would collect all the animals, a strange thing happened. Animals, birds, and insects of all varieties came to Noah. And, two by two, the creatures followed Noah into the Ark.

When the last one was inside, God closed the door.

The watching people were still jeering, but it had already begun to rain. The rain poured down like water from a bucket. The water rose higher than the mountaintops. Every living thing on the earth was destroyed as God had said it would be. But the Ark floated safely on the water with Noah and all the creatures snug and dry inside.

For forty days and forty nights, it rained. Then the rain stopped.

Noah looked out the window, but saw nothing except water.

After one hundred and fifty days, the Ark settled onto solid ground with a bump and a scrape.

"Surely we can get out now," said Noah's sons Shem, Ham, and Japheth.

But from the window, there was still nothing to be seen but water.

"We must be on a mountaintop," said Noah. "We shall have to wait longer yet." And they went on with the task of keeping the animals alive.

For over two months more, they waited. Now other mountaintops were showing. Noah took a raven and a dove and let them fly from the window. The raven flew to and fro until the earth was dry, but the dove returned to the Ark, having found no place to rest.

Seven days they waited. Once more Noah let the dove fly from the window. This time it returned carrying an olive leaf. "See," said Noah, "olive trees grow in the valleys. There must be dry land."

Everyone laughed and cheered. Seven more days they waited before Noah let the dove fly again. This time it did not return.

Cautiously, Noah opened the door of the Ark. He saw that the ground was dry. Then God said, "It is time to come out of the Ark: you, your family, and all the creatures."

So out came Noah. And out came all the animals, stretching and blinking in the sunshine before flying, galloping, hopping, scampering, and crawling away to make new homes and families.

The world was clean, shining, and beautiful again. Noah and his family built an altar, and Noah made a special thanksgiving offering to God for saving their lives.

God was pleased. He blessed Noah and his family and said, "You must have many children and fill the earth with people. Never again will I bring a great flood on the earth to destroy everything."

And then across the sky, Noah and his family saw an arc of beautiful colors shining against the dark clouds. God said, "This rainbow is a sign of my covenant. And whenever you see it, you can remember my promise. And my promise will last forever."

Tower of Babel

After the flood, Noah's sons and daughters-in-law had children, and their children had children, and so on, until Noah, who was by now a very old man, had a very large family with many great-great-grandchildren. The families began to spread out and wandered east looking for a good place to settle. They stopped at the plain of Shinar.

There they decided to build a splendid city with a huge tower at its center. The tower would be so high that it would reach right up to heaven. It would show everybody what an important nation this was.

The people started to build and the tower began to rise high. But God saw that the people were growing proud and arrogant. They had left him out of their lives and were trying to reach heaven by their own work. Soon they would be no better than the people before the flood had been. He had to stop them. So he did.

One morning when the people came to work, they found they couldn't understand what anyone else was saying. God had confused their language. The sounds came out all mixed up. No matter how much the people shouted or stamped their feet, they couldn't make themselves understood. Work on the tower stopped.

After a while, each person discovered a few others speaking a language which he or she could understand. These groups got together and moved away from the rest.

So God's purpose was fulfilled. The people were scattered over the earth.

The unfinished tower became known as the Tower of Babel because in Hebrew "Babel" means "confusion."

Abram

Abram was a brave man, ready to fight if the need arose, ready to do anything which God asked of him.

Abram had been living in the city of Ur, but the people there didn't worship the true God as Abram did. Abram's father, Terah, took his grandson Lot, Abram, and Abram's wife Sarai, and left Ur. They traveled to Haran where Terah died.

There God said, "Abram, I want you to leave here and go to a land which I will show you. I will bless you and your children and your children's children, and you shall become a great nation. You shall be a blessing to all who bless you. But those who curse you, I will curse."

Abram hesitated—leave everything he knew and set out on a journey with no idea of where it would end? But he loved God and believed God's promises. And soon a long procession of family, servants, goats, and sheep set out with Abram leading the way. No one knew where they were going. They all followed Abram, and Abram went where God told him.

Each night they camped, and each day they traveled. When they came to Shechem in Canaan, God said, "Abram, this is the land I will one day give to your children."

So far, Abram and Sarai had no children. And even though Abram was seventy-five years old, he still believed God's promises. He stopped and built an altar to the Lord.

There was a famine in the land, so Abram traveled on toward Egypt. But he was worried. Sarai was very beautiful. He was afraid the Egyptians would want her to be the wife of their ruler, Pharaoh. Abram was also afraid that they would kill him because he was her husband. So Abram decided to tell them Sarai was his sister.

Sarai agreed to the plan. It wasn't quite a lie because she was Abram's half-sister. When they reached Egypt, things happened as

Abram had expected. Pharaoh took Sarai to live in the palace and sent Abram, whom he thought was Sarai's brother, many rich gifts.

But God was not pleased with the deceit. He made Pharaoh and all his household very ill. Pharaoh soon realized the cause of the illness. He ordered Abram, Sarai, and Lot to leave the country at once, but he allowed Abram to keep all the gifts he had given him. Thankful to escape so lightly, Abram obeyed.

So as the long caravan set out again, Abram was a rich man.

Lot Is Captured

Abram and his nephew Lot now owned many sheep and cattle. It was hard to find enough food and water for all of the animals and people.

"Lot," Abram said, "let's separate. You choose which way you want to go, and I'll go the other way."

Lot was amazed that Abram, the leader, should give him first choice. Lot looked around and saw the rich, green grass of the plain with the River Jordan flowing through it. There would be no problem there with grazing or water. Lot quickly chose the plain. He took his people and his animals and went to live near the town of Sodom, although the people there were known to be very wicked.

Abram and his people stayed in Canaan, and God was pleased. God said to Abram as they stood on the high mountain, "Look in every direction. Everything that you can see I will give to you and to your offspring, who shall be too many to be counted."

So Abram built an altar of thanksgiving to God at Hebron and settled there.

Some time later, the kings of the plain of Jordan were attacked and defeated by four neighboring kings. Lot and his family were captured.

A messenger brought Abram the news. Abram didn't hesitate. He gathered his men and set off to rescue Lot.

When Abram and his men finally caught up with the enemy, he could see that they were heavily outnumbered. Abram planned a surprise attack. He divided his men so that the enemy was surrounded. That night they rushed the camp. In the darkness and confusion, the enemy was badly defeated. They fled in fear, leaving behind all their possessions and their captives. Lot and his family were saved, and Abram was declared a hero.

Returning from the defeated enemy's camp, Abram saw Melchizedek, the king of Salem and a priest of God Most High, coming out to meet them. This was a very great honor. Melchizedek brought out bread and wine, and he blessed Abram. Then Abram gave Melchizedek one tenth of all the riches the enemy had left behind.

Later the king of Sodom offered to share the remaining riches with Abram, but Abram refused. He wanted nothing from Sodom because of the wickedness of its people. After giving a portion to his men, Abram returned the remaining riches to the king of Sodom.

Once more God was pleased with Abram. He appeared to Abram, who was ninety-nine, and said, "I will make my covenant, my agreement, with you. I will bless you, and you will be the father of many nations. Your name shall no longer be Abram, but you shall be called Abraham. Your wife's name shall be Sarah, and I will bless her also. And she will be a mother of many nations."

GENESIS 18:32–33; 19:1–29

Escape from Sodom

Abraham pleaded with God, who was planning to destroy the cities of
Sodom and Gomorrah because of the wickedness of the people who
lived there. "If you find only ten good people in Sodom, will you
spare it?" begged Abraham.

"For only ten good people, I will spare the city," God promised.
And he sent two angels as messengers to inspect Sodom.

The angels looked like ordinary men. It was evening as they
entered Sodom, but Lot, who had been sitting by the gate, noticed
them. Knowing they were new to the town, he invited them to come
to his home for food and a place to stay as was the custom. When
they began to refuse, Lot insisted.

At his home, Lot sent for water to bathe their feet and had a meal
prepared for the visitors. They were still awake when the men of
Sodom came banging on the door of Lot's house.

"Bring out your visitors," shouted the men. "We want to amuse
ourselves with them."

Lot began to tremble, because he knew the men meant evil. He
went out to them, shutting the door behind him and tried to calm the
men of Sodom.

"Please, my friends, don't harm these men," he said. "They are
my guests and under my protection. Leave them in peace."

The men of Sodom did not listen to him. They charged forward
toward Lot, but the angels in the house quickly opened the door,
pulled Lot inside, and slammed the door just in time.

Then the angels blinded the men of Sodom so that they couldn't
see where the door was.

As the men wandered around outside, bewildered and afraid, the
messengers spoke urgently to Lot. "You must escape! This town must
be destroyed. Is there anyone else here who belongs to your family?
You must all run for your lives."

Lot rushed out to warn his sons-in-law. But they wouldn't listen.

"Hurry!" called the messengers as Lot came back alone.

Still Lot stood hesitating. Then one messenger grabbed the hands of Lot and his wife while the other seized the hands of Lot's two daughters, hurrying them out of town. Light was dawning.

"Run for the mountains and don't stop," the messengers ordered, preparing to leave Lot and his family.

"Not the mountains!" gasped Lot. "We'll never reach them in time. Let us take shelter in Zoar."

Zoar was a small town not far away.

The messengers agreed, but warned Lot and his family to run quickly and not look back.

Shaking and exhausted, Lot and his daughters reached Zoar as the sun was fully risen. Then God rained down sulphur and fire on Sodom and Gomorrah. The towns were totally destroyed.

Lot and his daughters were safe. But in spite of the warning, Lot's wife had stopped and looked back. And as she stood there gazing, she was turned into a pillar of salt.

Early the next morning, Abraham looked out where Sodom and Gomorrah had been, but all he could see was thick smoke billowing up from the plain. He knew that God had destroyed the towns. But God had remembered Abraham, and for his sake, God had saved Abraham's nephew Lot.

Abraham's Son, Isaac

Some months after Sodom was destroyed, Abraham was sitting in the doorway of his tent, trying to keep out of the hot midday sun.

When he looked up, Abraham saw three men standing nearby. He invited them to rest in the shade of the trees. The men accepted the invitation. His servants brought cool water to bathe their feet. Then Abraham rushed around organizing everything. His servants hurried to prepare food for them. Sarah, Abraham's wife, baked fresh bread.

Presently the men sat under the trees enjoying the meal. Sarah could overhear the conversation. "Where is your wife?" the men asked.

"She is in the tent," Abraham answered. By now, he was beginning to realize that these were no ordinary visitors.

One of the visitors said, "Before the year passes and I come again, Sarah will have a son."

A son? At her age? Sarah laughed aloud. She and Abraham were old, and Sarah had given up hope of having any children.

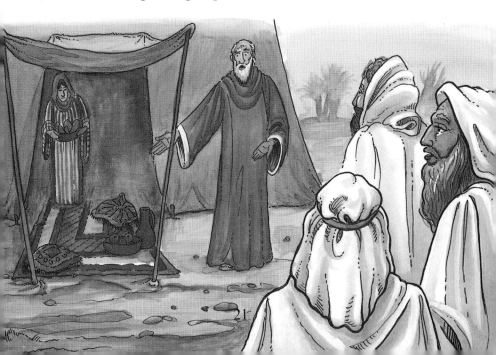

But in due time, God kept his promise, and Sarah did have a son. Abraham named him Isaac, or "Laughter."

Abraham and Sarah loved the boy very much. Indeed, as the child grew, God decided to test Abraham's obedience.

"Abraham," said God, "take your son to the mountains, and there offer him up as a sacrifice."

Sacrifice his son? Abraham wanted to cry out, No! No!

Yet Abraham had loved and obeyed God all his life.

So early the next morning, Abraham rose. With a heavy heart, he prepared his donkey for the journey, loading it with enough wood to make a fire for the burnt offering. Then he called to Isaac and two of his servants. "We are going to the mountains to make a sacrifice," he told them.

Isaac was excited as he set out beside his father.

After three days, Abraham saw they were near the place which God had told him about. He ordered his servants to stay with the donkey.

Abraham forced himself to unload the wood and gave it to Isaac to carry. He carried the fire and the knife.

At first Isaac walked happily beside his father. Then he said, "Father, you have the knife and I have the wood. But where is the

22

lamb we will offer?"

Abraham was shaken, but he managed to answer, "God will provide the lamb."

They walked on until they reached the place God had told Abraham about. Slowly, heavily, Abraham built an altar and arranged the wood. Now there were no more preparations to make. He could put the moment off no longer.

With eyes full of tears, he took Isaac, bound him with rope, and laid him on the altar. Abraham took the knife, ready to kill his son.

But just as his hand was raised to strike, an angel of the Lord called from heaven. "Stop! Don't harm the boy, for now I know you truly love and trust God. You were ready to offer your beloved son."

Isaac was safe. Trembling with relief, Abraham freed the lad. A ram was caught by the horns in a nearby thornbush, so Abraham offered the ram as a thanksgiving to God. He named the place The-Lord-Will-Provide.

Together he and Isaac went back to the waiting servants and home.

Rebecca

Abraham was very old now. He wanted to see his son Isaac happily married before he died. So he sent for his most trusted servant.

"Go to Mesopotamia, where I was born, and choose a wife for Isaac from among my own people," Abraham said.

This was a big responsibility. The servant was worried. "Suppose I choose a woman who won't come back with me?" he asked. "Shall I take Isaac there?"

"Oh no," Abraham said quickly. "God made a covenant, an agreement, with me that this land shall be given to my children and to their children. I don't want Isaac to go and live in Mesopotamia."

So the next day the servant set out. He took a few more servants and ten camels with him, for he had a plan.

It was beginning to get dark as he came to the city in Mesopotamia where Abraham's brother Nahor lived. Just outside the city was a well where the women came to draw water every evening. Here the servant stopped and prayed to God, "Please help me choose well. I will say to one of the girls, 'Will you give me a drink of water?' If she answers, 'Yes, and I'll give your camels a drink also,' I'll know she's the one you've chosen to be Isaac's wife."

The servant had hardly finished his prayer when the beautiful young girl Rebecca came walking along the path to the well.

Was this the right girl? The servant stammered, "Ah, ah, will you give me a drink of water?"

"Of course," she said and smiled. "I'll give your camels a drink as well." She drew water from the well until all the camels were satisfied. Now the servant knew this was the girl God had chosen. But there was still a doubt. Would she leave her home and family to marry a stranger?

The servant took out some gold to show he could pay for lodgings.

"Whose daughter are you?" he asked. "Is there room in your father's house for myself and the others to stay the night?"

"My father's name is Bethuel, son of Nahor," she replied. "We have plenty of room."

Bethuel, son of Nahor—the servant felt joy rising within him. God had brought him to the family of Abraham's brother!

Rebecca ran to tell her family what had happened at the well. Her brother Laban came down to speak to the servant. When Laban saw the servant's gold, he warmly invited the servant to lodge with them.

There the servant told them the whole story, explaining about Isaac. "And now," he finished, "if Rebecca will not come with me, please tell me."

Laban and Bethuel did not hesitate. "This is God's will," they said. "We will give permission for Rebecca to marry Isaac."

What a relief! The servant praised God. Then he brought out many rich gifts which he gave to Rebecca and to her mother and brother.

In the morning, the servant and his men were ready to leave. But Rebecca's mother and brother pleaded, "Please let her stay with us for just a few more days."

But the servant insisted he must return to his master.

Then they called Rebecca. "Will you go with this man?" they asked.

Bravely Rebecca replied, "Yes, I will."

So Rebecca and her servants with Abraham's servant and his men set out riding on the camels.

All this time Isaac had been waiting, wondering what sort of wife the servant would bring him. One evening as he went out in the field to pray, he saw the camel train approaching.

Rebecca looked across the field and saw Isaac. She slipped down from her camel. "Who is that?" she asked.

"My master's son," replied the servant.

As Isaac came running, Rebecca veiled her face, as was the custom. The servant told Isaac all that had happened.

Isaac took Rebecca into his mother's tent. She had died a very old woman, and Isaac had been very sad. But now Isaac and Rebecca were married. They loved one another and Isaac was comforted.

GENESIS 25:20–34; 27:1–45; 28:1–5

Isaac's Twin Sons

After a while Isaac and Rebecca had twin sons, Esau and Jacob. Esau had been born first so he was considered the older brother. The two boys were completely different from each other. As they grew up, Esau was always out in the wild. He became a skillful hunter. Jacob preferred to devote himself to the family business. Esau soon became their father's favorite; Jacob became their mother's favorite.

Many years later, after Isaac had become old and blind, he called to Esau, his favorite son. "My son, go hunting and bring back some game to make me my favorite dishes. Then bring them to me yourself so I can eat and give you my blessing before I die."

Rebecca overheard this. She watched Esau set out, then she hurried to Jacob. "Quickly! Go to our flock and get two of the best kids of the goats. I will cook your father's favorite dishes. Then you take them to him, pretending to be Esau. He will bless you instead of Esau."

So Jacob obeyed his mother. He brought back two of the best kids from the flock, which she then made into his father's favorite dishes. Next she put Esau's best clothes on Jacob, covering his hands and neck with the skins of the goats so that his skin would seem rough like Esau's.

Jacob went to his father. "Who's there?" called Isaac.

"It is your firstborn son, Esau," Jacob answered.

Isaac was puzzled. "How did you manage to find the animal so quickly?" he asked.

Jacob thought fast. "God helped me," he said.

Isaac was still puzzled. "Come close. Let me touch you," he said.

Jacob's heart thumped as the old man reached out and felt his hands and neck.

"The voice is Jacob's voice," said Isaac, "yet the hands are those of Esau."

So Isaac ate the meal. When he was finished eating, he gave Jacob the blessing which should have been given to the firstborn son, Esau.

"May God make you prosper. Let people serve you and let nations bow down to you. Be lord over your brothers, and let them bow down to you. Cursed be everyone who curses you, and blessed be everyone who blesses you."

Jacob left his father's tent. Hardly had he gone when Esau came back from hunting. He also had made his father's favorite foods and took them to him. "My father," he said, "eat this food so that you may bless me."

"What?" cried Isaac. Shaking, he sat up. "Who are you?" he asked.

"I'm Esau, your firstborn son," Esau answered in surprise.

Isaac could hardly speak. "Then who came to me just now? Who have I blessed? And he shall be blessed, for the blessing cannot be taken away."

Esau realized what had happened and wept. "Haven't you more

than one blessing to give?"

"You will prosper and serve your brother," Isaac answered. "But later you will free yourself from him."

Now Esau hated Jacob and determined to kill him as soon as Isaac died.

When Rebecca heard this, she was afraid for her favorite son, Jacob. "Go and stay with my brother, Laban," she said. "As soon as Esau forgets what has happened, I'll send a messenger. Then you can come home."

Jacob, who was quite frightened, prepared to leave. But before he left, Isaac called for Jacob to further bless and charge him.

"My son, do not marry a woman from Canaan. Marry one of the daughters of Laban. And may God bless you so that you will inherit the land, as he promised to Abraham."

Comforted a little, Jacob set out.

Jacob's Dream

All alone, Jacob started out on his journey from Beersheba to Haran where his uncle, Laban, lived. Jacob hurried along, afraid his brother Esau would come after him to kill him.

As it began to grow dark, Jacob knew he would have to rest. He found a stone which he could use as a pillow and lay down. He then pulled his thick cloak around him for a blanket. Exhausted, he soon fell asleep.

That night Jacob had a dream. In his dream he saw a ladder reaching from the ground nearby right up into heaven. Angels were going up and down the ladder, and at the top stood the Lord God himself.

God spoke to Jacob and said, "I am the God of Abraham and of Isaac. The land on which you lie I will give to you and to your children and to your children's children. Your descendants shall be like the dust of the earth. And they shall spread to the west and to the

east, to the north and to the south. Through you and your family, all the people of the earth will be blessed. And behold, I am with you and will keep you in all places to which you go, and I will bring you again to this land. For I will not leave you until I have done everything I have promised."

Jacob awoke. He looked around. The land was still and quiet in the starlight. But Jacob was afraid, in spite of God's comforting message.

"Surely this is God's house and the gate of heaven, and I didn't know it," he said.

As soon as it was light, he took the stone he had used as a pillow and stood it up on one end to make a pillar. He poured oil over the stone and called the place Bethel, which means "The House of God." Then he made a promise.

"If God is with me to guard me and keep me, if he will give me bread to eat and clothing to wear, and if he will bring me safely back to my father's house," Jacob vowed, "then the Lord God will be my God. And of all that God gives to me, I will surely give a tenth back to him."

Jacob Works for Laban

Jacob traveled on and at last he came to a well with a huge stone over its mouth. From the nearby shepherds Jacob learned that Laban's daughter Rachel was bringing the sheep for water.

Jacob looked at Rachel as she came down the path. She was very beautiful. He hurried to move the heavy stone which covered the well. Then he drew the water for Laban's sheep while Rachel watched, puzzled but grateful.

When the sheep were satisfied, Jacob greeted Rachel with a kiss and explained who he was. Rachel ran to tell her father. Laban came hurrying out to welcome Jacob and bring him back home.

Jacob explained all that had happened. Laban agreed that Jacob could stay in spite of what had happened.

Jacob began to work for Laban. After a month Laban said, "It's not right that you should work for nothing even if I am your uncle. What would you like your wages to be?"

By now Jacob loved Rachel very much. So he said, "I will gladly work for seven years without pay if at the end of that time, I can marry Rachel, your youngest daughter."

32

Laban had two daughters. Normally the eldest, Leah, would be given in marriage first. But Laban said, "It is better that you should marry Rachel than a stranger."

Jacob worked hard for seven years, at which time Laban arranged a wedding. But in the evening, when it was time for the bride to go to her husband, Laban brought Leah to Jacob's tent, not Rachel.

In the morning, when Jacob discovered the trick, he was furious. Laban told him if he would work another seven years, he could marry Rachel. At that time men often had more than one wife, so both sisters could be married to Jacob.

So Jacob worked another seven years for Rachel. He always loved Rachel more than Leah.

Jacob had several children by Leah and their two maidservants, but Rachel was unhappy because she had none. She prayed to God, and at last a baby boy was born to her. They called the boy Joseph, and he was Jacob's favorite son.

Jacob had now stayed with Laban for twenty years and had grown rich. Laban's sons grew jealous and even Laban was not as friendly as he had once been.

One day God spoke to Jacob. "Go back to your own land. I will be with you."

Jacob was afraid his uncle would not let him go, so he waited until Laban was away shearing the sheep. Then he collected all his family, his servants, his cattle, his sheep, and his possessions, and he fled. Unknown to Jacob, Rachel had stolen her father's household idols.

When Laban discovered that Jacob had gone, he was furious. He set out with the men of his family in pursuit. Finally he caught sight of Jacob's tents on the mountain.

God spoke to Laban. "Be careful what you say to Jacob."

Still angry, Laban pitched his tents near Jacob's camp, then he rushed off to find him. Trembling, Jacob faced his uncle.

"Why did you leave without letting me say good-bye to my daughters and my grandchildren?" Laban roared. "I could kill you, but God has told me to be careful what I say to you."

Jacob felt a little better.

But Laban was shouting again. "Why did you steal my idols?"

Jacob was truly innocent. "I haven't stolen them," he said. "If anyone here did steal them, that person shall die. Search the camp."

Laban searched Jacob's tent and the servants' tents without finding anything. Then he came to Rachel's tent. Instead of coming to greet her father, Rachel sat on the cushions which had been on her camel, saying she didn't feel well.

Laban searched her tent. He found nothing.

Jacob protested angrily, but Laban was equally angry. They decided to make a covenant, an agreement. So they set up a stone for a pillar and agreed that Laban would not cross to the land on Jacob's side and that Jacob would not cross to the land on Laban's side. Then Jacob made a sacrifice to God.

Laban never discovered that Rachel had stolen his household idols and had hidden them by sitting on them throughout the entire search.

Jacob and Esau Meet

Jacob was safe from Laban. Now he began to worry about meeting his brother Esau. The last time they had been together, Esau had threatened to kill him.

Jacob sent messengers to tell Esau he was returning and hoped for friendship. The messengers soon came hurrying back. "Esau is coming to meet you with four hundred men," they reported.

Jacob was terrified. Thinking Esau planned to attack him, Jacob quickly divided his camp into two groups, so that at least one group might escape. Then he prayed to God, begging him to save them.

That night Jacob collected 220 sheep, 220 goats, 30 camels and their young, 50 head of cattle, and 30 donkeys to use as a peace offering to his brother. Each group was to be driven separately by his servants to Esau as a gift. To the first servant he said, "Tell Esau, 'These are your servant Jacob's. Take these as a present from him.' Tell him I am coming behind you."

Jacob sent the next servant with the same message, and so on, until all were on their way.

By the time Esau has received all my gifts, he may no longer be angry, Jacob thought anxiously.

He sent his two wives, two maidservants, and eleven sons to the other side of the brook.

Now it was dark and Jacob was alone with his fear. Suddenly, a stranger came and wrestled with him. All night they struggled, but Jacob would not give in.

As morning dawned, the stranger said, "Your name shall no longer be Jacob. You shall be called Israel because you have struggled with God and with men and have overcome. Now let me go."

Exhausted, Jacob obeyed. "Tell me your name," he gasped.

But the stranger replied, "Why do you ask my name?" and blessed Jacob.

Then Jacob called that place Penuel, and he declared, "I believe I have fought with God face to face and yet lived."

Now the sun rose high. Jacob looked up and saw Esau coming.

Hastily Jacob, his wives, and children moved toward his twin brother.

When Jacob neared Esau, he stopped and bowed low seven times. But Esau ran to meet Jacob, throwing his arms around him and kissing him.

And from then on, the two brothers were friends.

Joseph the Dreamer

Joseph, the son of Jacob and Rachel, had ten older half brothers, and none of them liked him. The family was living in Canaan now, and Joseph was old enough to help his brothers care for the animals and cultivate the land. Joseph's brothers knew he was their father's favorite, and they were jealous.

Jacob made Joseph a coat of many colors, which the boy loved and wore all the time. His brothers wore rough tunics, and they hated Joseph with his fine coat.

If his brothers were slow in finishing their work, Joseph told his father. Then his brothers hated him all the more.

One night Joseph dreamed a dream which he told to his brothers. "We were all in the fields, binding up the sheaves of grain. And my sheaf stood up straight while all of yours bowed down to it."

His brothers were furious. "Do you think we shall ever bow down to you?" they said.

Then Joseph had another dream. This time he told it to his brothers and his father.

"In my dream, the sun, the moon, and eleven stars bowed down to me," he said.

Even his father was not very pleased, "Shall I, your mother, and your brothers really bow down to you?" he asked.

One day Jacob said to Joseph, "Your brothers have been away a very long time with the flocks. Go see if anything's wrong. They'll be near Shechem."

So Joseph set out. He reached Shechem safely, but there was no sign of his brothers or the animals. A man told him his brothers had gone to Dothan, so Joseph went toward Dothan.

Before Joseph reached his brothers, they looked up and saw him coming. They began plotting to kill him.

One of the brothers, Reuben, didn't want to harm Joseph, but he knew it was no use trying to dissuade his brothers while they were in this mood. He thought quickly. "If we kill him, it will mean we have shed his blood. Let's just throw him into the pit and leave him," he suggested. "Joseph will never be able to climb out. He will die there."

The others agreed. But secretly Reuben planned to rescue Joseph while the others weren't there.

Joseph came up to his brothers and greeted them. Immediately they seized him, tore off his coat of many colors, and threw him into the pit. Then they sat down to enjoy a meal. Bewildered and afraid, Joseph prayed to God for comfort and help.

Judah, another of the brothers, looked over toward the road. He saw a camel caravan approaching. The camels were loaded with spices to sell in Egypt. Now Reuben was not with them at this moment.

"Hey!" Judah exclaimed. "Let's sell Joseph as a slave to these Midianite traders. That way we will not have laid a hand on him. He is, after all, our brother. We shall be rid of him, and we'll have some money in exchange."

The others agreed. Roughly they hauled Joseph out of the pit. Joseph was young, strong, and good-looking. The Midianites bought him gladly, paying his brothers twenty pieces of silver.

The traders bound Joseph with rope and continued on their journey. Joseph's brothers returned to their flocks.

Meanwhile, Reuben had come back. He stole over to the pit and found it empty. Reuben tore his clothes in grief.

"The boy isn't here! What am I going to do?" he cried. His brothers told the story to Reuben. There was nothing he could do to help Joseph then.

The brothers dipped Joseph's torn coat into the blood of one of their goats. They took the coat back to their father, saying they had found it on the path.

Jacob cried out, "My son has been torn into pieces by wild animals!" He wept and no one could comfort him.

Joseph, Potiphar, and Prison

Now Joseph was alone, friendless in a foreign land. He was sold as a slave to Potiphar, who was captain of the guard and one of Pharaoh's officers. But God had not forgotten Joseph.

At first Joseph was given all the heaviest work to do. But he worked willingly and well. Potiphar soon realized that Joseph could be trusted. Joseph was made chief servant of the household and was allowed to move about freely.

Just as Joseph's life was becoming easier, Potiphar's wife noticed him. She desired him and asked him to lie with her.

Joseph refused and, as he ran from her, she grabbed his garment.

Potiphar's wife was furious. She went to Potiphar, seeking revenge. "Your slave tried to force himself on me!" she said, holding up Joseph's garment. "When I screamed, he fled, leaving this behind!"

When he heard this, Potiphar was angry. He refused to give Joseph a chance to explain and had him thrown into prison.

But God was still with Joseph. Even in prison, Joseph's quiet

strength and clear mind were soon recognized. Before long, the warden put Joseph in charge of the other prisoners.

When he had been in prison for a while, two of Pharaoh's servants, the chief butler and the chief baker, angered Pharaoh. They were put in the same prison as Joseph, and they were in his charge.

One morning he found them looking very worried.

"We both had strange dreams last night," they told him. "There's no one here to explain what they mean."

"Tell me your dreams, and God will help me to interpret them," said Joseph.

The chief butler spoke first. "In my dream, I saw a vine with three branches. It grew buds which blossomed and ripened into grapes. I took some of the grapes and squeezed their juice into Pharaoh's cup. Then I took the cup and gave it to Pharaoh."

Joseph said, "The three branches stand for three days. Before three days are over, Pharaoh will send for you and return you to your position as chief butler. When you stand in front of Pharaoh, please tell him about me. Tell him I have done nothing wrong."

The butler promised he would, for he was very pleased.

The chief baker heard the good interpretation of the butler's dream, and he hurried to tell his own dream. "There were three baskets resting on my head, one on top of the other. The top basket was full of all kinds of fresh goods that I had baked for Pharaoh. But birds were flying down and eating from the top basket."

Then Joseph spoke sadly. "The three baskets also stand for three days. Within three days, Pharaoh will send for you. But he will hang you from a tree, and when you are dead, the birds will eat your flesh."

The baker was terrified. After three days, Pharaoh sent for the butler and the baker. He returned the butler to his old position, but he hanged the baker, just as Joseph had said.

The butler, safely out of prison, forgot all about Joseph until one night when Pharaoh himself had a dream.

Pharaoh Dreams

Pharaoh sent for all his wise men. He was worried. "I have had two dreams," he said. "In the first, I was standing by the River Nile when seven fat cows came out of the water and began to graze on the riverbank. As I watched, seven thin cows followed them out of the water, and the thin cows ate the fat cows."

Pharaoh shivered. Then he went on. "In my second dream, I saw seven good ears of corn growing on one stalk. Then seven thin ears of corn sprouted on the stalk and swallowed up the good ears. What do these dreams mean?"

But the wise men were not able to interpret the dreams.

Then the chief butler remembered Joseph. He hurried to Pharaoh. "Sir, when I was in prison, I had a dream. The chief baker also had a dream. A young man was there who told us what our dreams meant."

"Bring him to me at once!" ordered Pharaoh.

A messenger ran to the prison.

Hardly able to believe it, Joseph soon found himself in the palace, standing in front of Pharaoh.

Pharaoh said, "I have heard that you can interpret dreams."

"I cannot do it," Joseph replied steadily. "But my God will tell me what your dreams mean."

"Very well," said Pharaoh. Once more he told his dreams.

Joseph listened. Then he said, "The two dreams have the same meaning. God has shown you what he plans to do. The seven fat cows and the seven good ears of corn mean that Egypt will have seven years when the harvests are good. But the seven thin cows and the seven thin ears of corn mean that the good years will be followed by seven years of famine."

Pharaoh was shaken. Seven years of famine! What would happen to Egypt?

Joseph went on. "God has shown you this so that the people need

not starve. You must find a good, trustworthy man and put him in charge of all Egypt to see that your orders are carried out. You should command that during the seven good years, one fifth of all the grain be stored in barns. When the seven years of famine come, there will be enough food stored to keep the people alive. But even then the food must be distributed with care."

Pharaoh began to smile. "This is a good plan. Since it is through you that God has spoken and since in all Egypt I know of no one wiser than you, you shall be in charge."

Joseph's time of hardship was over. Now everyone recognized Joseph and bowed to him.

During the seven years of good harvests, Joseph traveled throughout Egypt, making sure that a fifth of the grain was stored.

When the first years of famine came, Joseph ordered that the grain stores should be opened. People from miles around came to Egypt to buy grain, for there was famine everywhere.

Journey into Egypt

Grain for Joseph's Brothers

There was famine in Canaan. Jacob called his sons together and said to them, "There is grain in Egypt. Go and buy some."

So Joseph's ten older brothers set out. Jacob wouldn't allow Benjamin, the youngest, to go, for fear harm would come to him.

The journey was long. At last, weary, travel-stained, and hungry, Joseph's brothers arrived in Egypt. They came to Joseph and bowed low in front of him, begging that they might buy grain.

Joseph recognized them at once. Here were the brothers who had sold him as a slave, the brothers whom he had dreamed would one day bow down to him.

But Joseph's brothers did not recognize their younger brother.

Joseph didn't mean to give himself away just yet. He spoke to them in Egyptian through an interpreter.

"You haven't really come for food. You are spies!" Joseph accused roughly.

"No, no," his brothers replied fearfully. "We have only come to buy food. We are ten of twelve sons from the same father. One brother is at home and much younger. The other brother is no more. If we do not get grain, our family will starve."

When Joseph heard that his father and younger brother were still alive, he longed to see them. But how could it be managed?

"You are spies," Joseph insisted. "I won't believe anything you say unless you show me this younger brother. You must go back home and bring him to Egypt, and one of you shall be imprisoned here until you all return."

He then had them all put in prison for three days.

On the third day, Joseph went to his brothers to see what their decision was. He found them greatly distressed. They spoke to one another, unaware that he understood what they were saying.

"This is our punishment for showing Joseph no mercy," they said.

Joseph had to hide his tears, but he spoke to them as harshly as before. One of the brothers, Simeon, was left behind as a hostage.

With heavy hearts the others set out, their donkeys loaded with grain. Secretly, Joseph had ordered that their money should be returned. Each man's money was hidden in his sack of grain.

When the brothers later discovered the money, they were puzzled and uneasy. Finally, they reached home. But they had to tell their father that Simeon had been left behind in Egypt because the young ruler there wanted to see Benjamin. It was all very strange.

But Jacob would not even consider letting Benjamin go.

The grain from Egypt lasted for a while, then starvation faced them once more. Jacob finally allowed Benjamin to leave.

Joseph was sure his brothers would return. When at last he saw them and saw that Benjamin was with them, he was overjoyed. But

still he did not tell them who he was. "Bring those men to my house," he ordered his servants. "Bring Simeon also. We shall have a feast."

The brothers were afraid. They began to explain that they didn't steal the money the first time, and they brought double payment this time. They brought gifts as well. They also brought their younger brother, just as they'd been ordered.

Joseph answered them kindly, telling them not to worry. They all sat down to a splendid meal.

After the meal, the sacks were loaded with grain. Joyfully the brothers set off on the journey back to Canaan.

But Joseph had again ordered that their money be returned and had also commanded that a silver cup be hidden in Benjamin's sack.

Joseph gave his brothers time to leave the town. Then he sent his steward after them, saying his valuable cup had been stolen and their sacks must be searched.

The brothers allowed the search, sure of their innocence. To their horror the cup was discovered, and Benjamin was ordered to return.

His brothers would not let him go back alone. In deep distress, they all returned. Bowing low before Joseph, they tried to explain.

Joseph said Benjamin must remain as a slave. The others were free to go.

This was too much. How could they tell Jacob that Benjamin was lost to him? Judah came forward. Humbly and desperately he pleaded with Joseph, confessing the way they had once ill-treated a younger brother. He described their father's grief at the loss of his son.

As Joseph listened, tears filled his eyes. "Leave us!" he ordered his servants.

"Don't be afraid," he said. "I am Joseph, the brother you sold. But I am not angry. Don't be angry with yourselves. God has been with me and sent me here so that your lives might be saved."

At first the brothers couldn't take it in. When they began to understand, they were overjoyed. Joseph was safe and they were forgiven.

"Now," said Joseph, "go back to Canaan and tell my father that I am alive. Tell him there will be five more years of famine, and bring him here to live with me."

Jacob Goes to Egypt

Pharaoh heard that Joseph's brothers were in Egypt. He sent for Joseph. "I'm glad your brothers have come," he said. "Let them go back to Canaan with plenty of grain. But also send enough carts to bring the whole family here, where they can live in plenty."

Gladly Joseph carried out Pharaoh's orders, and his brothers set out again.

At last the brothers reached home. Eagerly they hurried to tell their father the good news.

Jacob was a very old man now and could hardly take it in. His son Joseph was not dead? "I will go to Egypt. And I shall see my son again before I die," he cried joyfully.

Back in Egypt, Joseph had been waiting impatiently. When he heard that his brothers had reached Goshen, he could wait no longer. He ordered his chariot and hurried to meet them.

At last Jacob's arms were around his son once more.

Joseph took his father and five of his brothers and presented them to Pharaoh. Pharaoh welcomed them kindly and told Joseph to settle them in the fertile land of Goshen.

For some years Jacob lived happily in Egypt. When he died, Joseph and the brothers carried him back to Canaan to be buried next to Abraham and Sarah, Isaac and Rebecca, and Leah.

Joseph and all of his family remained in the land of Goshen in Egypt and were known as the Israelites.

Joseph lived long enough to see his grandchildren and his great-grandchildren. When he was very old, Joseph said to them, "Remember, God one day will bring you out of this land into the land which he has promised. The land he promised to Abraham, to Isaac, and to Jacob."

48

The Baby in the Bulrushes

Years passed. Joseph had died, as had the Pharaoh who had been so kind to the Israelites.

Now the Pharaoh who ruled in his place became afraid because there were so many Israelites in Egypt. "If there is a war, they might join with our enemies and fight against us," he said. "We must make them our slaves. Then they'll have no will or strength for a battle."

So life became hard for the Israelites. They were forced to work in the fields making bricks. They built the cities of Pithom and Raamses.

But Pharaoh's plan didn't work. The more the Israelites were beaten and ill-treated, the more they grew in strength and in numbers.

So Pharaoh ordered that every baby boy born to the Israelites should be drowned in the river. Girls would be allowed to live and become slaves.

One family could not bear to follow Pharaoh's orders. At first their baby boy slept most of the time, and it was easy to hide him. But as he grew, he slept less, and his cries became louder.

His mother, Jochebed, watched and worried. At last she thought of a plan.

She asked God to help her.

She then wove a basket-cradle and a lid from dried bulrushes. She covered the outside with pitch, so that it was waterproof and would float. Next she made the inside soft and cozy with blankets.

Then Jochebed laid the baby boy in the basket.

She took the basket and, along with her daughter Miriam, crept down to the river. Carefully Jochebed placed the basket in the water among the reeds.

"Hide nearby and watch," she told Miriam. Jochebed knew that every day the Pharaoh's daughter came to this part of the river to bathe. The baby would be found.

Jochebed prayed again to God.

With a fast-beating heart, Miriam crouched among the bulrushes, watching and waiting.

Presently she saw Pharaoh's daughter coming with her maids. Would the baby be discovered? Would Pharaoh's daughter have him drowned? Miriam clasped her hands tightly together.

Pharaoh's daughter saw the basket-cradle. "Bring that to me!" she commanded. A maid brought it to her and, as Pharaoh's daughter opened the lid, the baby cried.

"This is one of the Israelite babies," said Pharaoh's daughter with sorrow in her eyes.

Suddenly Miriam knew what to do. Scrambling to her feet, she ran forward. "Please, shall I find a nurse to look after the baby for you?" she gasped.

"Yes, go," said Pharaoh's daughter.

Eagerly Miriam rushed away and brought back her mother.

"Take care of this baby," Pharaoh's daughter ordered Jochebed. "I will pay you."

The baby's life was saved, and Jochebed was allowed to look after him openly for pay. It was better than she had ever hoped.

As the baby grew, Jochebed taught him about God and told him stories of Abraham, Isaac, and Jacob.

When he was old enough, Jochebed took him to Pharaoh's palace to live. Pharaoh's daughter named him Moses and treated him as if he were her own son.

Moses in the Land of Midian

Moses lived in the splendid palace of the Pharaoh, but he never forgot that he was an Israelite. As he grew up, he hated to see his own people forced to toil as slaves.

One day as he walked through the fields, he saw an Egyptian taskmaster cruelly beating an Israelite slave. Furious, Moses glanced around. There was no one else nearby. Moses struck the Egyptian, killing him. He quickly buried the body in the sand. Then he hurried on, thinking his deed would remain a secret.

The next day he saw two slaves fighting each other. "Stop that!" he shouted. "Why are you hitting one of your own countrymen?"

The men paused. One of them answered, "Who made you a judge over us? Are you going to kill me the way you killed that Egyptian?"

Moses was horrified. The slave must have told them. Everyone knows what I did, he thought. Someone is sure to report it to Pharaoh.

Pharaoh did indeed hear of it. He ordered that Moses be killed.

But Moses escaped, fleeing to the land of Midian. There, lonely and tired, he sat down by a well to rest.

Seven daughters of Jethro, the priest of a nearby village, came to the well to get water for their sheep. Moses idly watched. Some shepherds came along, all men. Roughly they told the girls to get out of the way until their sheep had been given a drink.

It wasn't fair. Angrily Moses sprang up. He made the men wait and helped the girls, drawing water for them himself until all their sheep were satisfied. The girls were amazed and delighted.

When they reached home, they told their father what had happened, and Moses was invited to stay with the family.

Moses agreed. After a while Jethro gave Moses his daughter Zipporah for a wife, and Moses became a shepherd.

But his people, the Israelites, were still in Egypt.

God had not forgotten them. He remembered the covenant he had made with Abraham, Isaac, and Jacob.

Moses and the Burning Bush

Moses now lived in the desert, caring for the sheep of his father-in-law, Jethro. One day while searching for pastures where the flock could graze, Moses came to Mount Horeb.

There he saw a most extraordinary thing.

On the mountainside a bush was on fire. Flames were shooting up, yet the bush did not burn. Cautiously Moses moved closer to have a better look. He jumped back as he heard a voice speaking to him from the burning bush.

"Moses, do not come any closer," the voice commanded. "Take off your shoes, for this is holy ground. I am God."

Moses shook with fear. Quickly he slipped off his sandals.

God spoke again. "I have chosen you to be the leader of the Israelites and to bring them out of Egypt."

"Me?" cried Moses. "But I'm nobody special. No one will take any notice of what I say."

"I will be with you," said God. "Tell the people the one who is called *I Am* has sent you."

Moses swallowed hard. "Suppose they still don't believe me?"

"Throw your rod to the ground," commanded God.

Puzzled, Moses obeyed. Instantly the rod turned into a writhing snake.

"Aah!" cried Moses as he ran from it.

"Pick it up," commanded God. "By the tail."

Moses stopped. Pick it up by the tail? That wasn't the way to pick up a snake—it could whip around and strike you.

Yet that was what God had commanded. So Moses forced himself to grab the snake by its tail.

The snake turned back into a rod in his hand.

God said, "Now put your hand inside your garment."

Moses obeyed. When he brought his hand out, it was white with the dreaded disease leprosy.

"Now put it back again," God ordered.

Again Moses obeyed. This time when he brought his hand out, the leprosy was gone.

"These are two miraculous signs by which you can prove I have spoken to you," said God. "If they still will not believe, here is a third sign. Take some water from the River Nile and pour it onto the ground. It will turn into blood."

Moses stood there by the burning bush and imagined himself in Egypt, speaking to the leaders of his own people and to Pharaoh.

"Lord," he pleaded, "I am not good at talking to people. Please send someone else."

God grew angry because Moses still didn't trust him. But he said, "Take your brother Aaron with you. He shall speak for you both. And take your rod. For you shall perform the signs. Then you shall lead my people out of Egypt."

Moses knew he must obey God and go to Egypt.

55

Pharaoh and the Israelite Slaves

Moses explained to Jethro why he must suddenly leave Midian.

Jethro understood. "Go in peace," he said.

Moses prepared for his journey. But he was very anxious. Would there still be trouble for him in Egypt because of the man he had killed?

God reassured him. "All the men who wanted to kill you are dead."

So that problem was solved. But there still remained the enormous task of leading the Israelites out of Egypt.

Still anxious, Moses set out, taking his wife and sons with him. God knew how Moses was feeling and sent his brother Aaron to meet him in the wilderness.

The two brothers greeted each other warmly, for it had been years since they had last seen each other. Then Moses told Aaron of the task which God had given them to do and of the miraculous signs which Moses was to perform as proof that God was with them.

Together Moses and Aaron went to the Israelites and called an assembly of the leaders. Aaron gave God's message, and Moses showed them the signs.

The Israelites believed and worshiped God. "God has not forgotten us," they cried. "We shall soon be free."

But first Pharaoh had to agree to set his slaves free.

Moses and Aaron stood in front of Pharaoh. Aaron said, "The God of Israel says, 'Let my people go so that they can hold a feast in the wilderness and make sacrifices to me there.'"

Pharaoh replied angrily, "Who is this God of Israel? Why should I do as he says? I will not let Israel go."

Pharaoh then ordered the Israelites to work harder than ever.

"Keep them busy. Then they'll have neither the time nor the energy to listen to stories of feast days and sacrifices."

The taskmasters obeyed Pharaoh. They no longer gave the Israelites the straw to make the bricks. Instead, the Israelites were forced to find their own straw. This took time. The slaves weren't able to make the same number of bricks as before, no matter how hard they toiled in the hot sun. As a result, they were beaten cruelly.

The leaders of the Israelites went to Pharaoh. "Why do you treat us so harshly?" they cried.

"Because you are lazy," Pharaoh answered. "All this talk of sacrificing to your God is just an excuse."

As the Israelite leaders left the palace, they met Moses and Aaron, who had been waiting anxiously outside.

"God will judge you," the leaders shouted angrily. "You have made things much worse for us. Now we'll either die from overwork or be beaten to death."

Moses became discouraged.

Then God said to Moses, "I will perform signs and miracles. The Egyptians shall know that I am God. Go back to Pharaoh and there do as I tell you."

The Plagues of Egypt

Once again Moses and Aaron were standing in front of Pharaoh.

"If I am to believe you bring a message from your God, show me a sign," said Pharaoh.

God had predicted Pharaoh would say this. Aaron was prepared. He threw down his rod which turned into a snake.

Pharaoh was not easily impressed. He sent for his magicians. They threw down their rods and magically turned them into snakes.

But Aaron's rod swallowed all the others.

Still Pharaoh wouldn't listen to Moses and Aaron. Discouraged and disappointed, they left the palace.

God spoke to Moses. "Pharaoh is very stubborn. This is what you must do. In the morning Pharaoh will go down to the River Nile. Wait for him on the bank. As he comes near, say, 'The Lord has sent me to tell you to let the Israelites go and worship in the desert. I will strike the waters of the Nile with my rod, and the river will turn into blood. This is how you will know he is God.'"

Moses listened, swallowing hard. God spoke again. "Then tell Aaron to hold out his rod, and all the rivers, canals, and ponds of Egypt shall turn into blood."

Moses and Aaron obeyed God, and it happened exactly as God had said.

Stubbornly Pharaoh sent for his magicians. They also turned water into blood by magic.

"There you are," said Pharaoh, and he went back to his palace.

The Egyptians had to dig for water along the banks of the river.

After a week went by and the waters were clearing, God said to Moses, "Go again to Pharaoh and tell him if he still refuses to let my people go, I will send a plague of frogs."

Moses and Aaron repeated God's message to Pharaoh. But Pharaoh was unmoved.

Aaron held out his rod and up from the River Nile came hundreds and thousands of frogs.

Then Pharaoh's magicians made even more frogs appear.

"You see?" said Pharaoh triumphantly. But really he couldn't stand all the frogs hopping out unexpectedly, frogs getting squashed underfoot, frogs croaking.

He sent for Moses and Aaron. "Ask your God to take these frogs away. Then I will let your people go to offer sacrifices in the wilderness."

Moses didn't obey immediately. "You may fix the time when I shall pray to God," he said. "And so that you will know it is God's work, when I pray, all the frogs will die except those in the river."

"Pray tomorrow," Pharaoh said, as if there were no hurry.

The next day Moses prayed to God, and the frogs died exactly as Moses had said. There were piles and piles of dead frogs. The whole land smelled of dead frogs.

Yet as soon as the frogs were gone, Pharaoh refused to let the Israelites go.

God said to Moses and Aaron, "Strike the dust of the ground with your rod, and all through Egypt the dust shall turn into gnats."

Moses and Aaron obeyed, and gnats sprang up everywhere. They zoomed around, biting both people and animals until all the Egyptians were scratching themselves.

Pharaoh's magicians could not make gnats appear.

"The gnats are a sign from God," they said, trembling. Still Pharaoh would not let the slaves go.

God spoke again to Moses. "Get up early tomorrow morning. Once more speak to Pharaoh as he goes to the river. Tell him that if he will not let my people go, the houses of the Egyptians will be filled with flies. But so that he will know I am God, there shall be no flies in Goshen where the Israelites live."

And so it happened. Pharaoh would not let the people go, and on the following day, swarms of flies filled his palace and all of Egypt— except in Goshen.

Pharaoh sent for Moses and Aaron. "You may sacrifice to your God," he cried. "But do it here, not in the wilderness."

"No," Moses answered. "Your people would be offended. They would throw stones at us. We must make a three-day journey into the wilderness to offer our sacrifices. This is what the Lord God commands."

The flies buzzed and zoomed around Pharaoh's head. "Oh, very well," he snapped. "You may go into the wilderness, but not far. Now pray to your God to take these flies away."

"As soon as I leave the palace, I will pray for you," Moses replied warily. "Tomorrow the flies will go, but the Pharaoh must keep his part of the bargain."

"Of course," said Pharaoh.

Moses left the palace and prayed to God.

The next day not one fly remained in Egypt. But as soon as Pharaoh realized there were no more flies, he refused to let the Israelites go.

Once more God sent Moses to warn Pharaoh. God would send a cattle disease so that all the Egyptian livestock would die. But the animals of the Israelites would be untouched. Once more Pharaoh refused to listen, and once more God did as he had said.

Still Pharaoh would not let the Israelites go.

Then God told Moses and Aaron to take handfuls of soot from the fire and throw it into the air in front of Pharaoh. When Moses and Aaron obeyed, boils broke out on all the people of Egypt. Yet still Pharaoh would not let the Israelites go.

Then God sent Moses with another message for Pharaoh. Moses spoke, "So that you may know his power, the Lord God will send a great storm. The people and the animals of Egypt should all get under cover, or they will be killed."

By now some of the Egyptians believed God would do as he said. These people hurried to get their families and animals indoors. But some people stayed out in the open as usual.

The storm came, and it was the worst storm Egypt had ever known. Every living thing out in the open was killed. Yet in Goshen there was no storm at all.

Pharaoh sent urgently for Moses and Aaron. As the lightning flashed and the thunder rolled, Pharaoh cried, "I know I've done wrong. Pray to your God. No more storms like this, please. You and your people can go at once."

Moses was still wary. "When I am outside the city, I will pray to God. The storms will stop so that you may know God's power. But I can see you still do not really believe in him."

Moses left the palace. Once outside the city, he prayed as he had promised. Immediately the rain, thunder, and lightning stopped.

But when Pharaoh realized the storm was over, he would not let the people go.

God comforted Moses. "Do not get too upset. I am performing these miracles so that you will be able to tell your children's children how I treated the Egyptians. Then they will know that I am indeed Lord. Now go and tell Pharaoh that if he does not let my people go, I will send a plague of locusts."

So once more Moses and Aaron stood in front of Pharaoh, giving him God's message. The Egyptian leaders were afraid. "Don't you see that Egypt is being ruined?" they cried. "Let the Israelites go and worship their God."

Pharaoh asked warily, "Who will go and worship your God in the wilderness?"

"Every one of us," replied Moses.

"No!" cried Pharaoh angrily. "Only the men may go." And he had Moses and Aaron thrown out of the palace.

God sent the locusts. The ground was black with them. They ate every leaf and every fruit in all the land of Egypt.

Once more Pharaoh begged Moses and Aaron to have the plague removed. Once more God removed it. But still Pharaoh would not let the Israelites go. Then God sent darkness over the land of Egypt for three whole days. Only the Israelites had daylight.

In fear, Pharaoh sent for Moses. "Go!" he cried. "Every one of you."

"We must also take our animals," said Moses.

"No!" stormed Pharaoh. "Get out of my palace. If I ever see you again, you shall die."

"Very well," retorted Moses.

Now God prepared to bring the worst plague of all to Egypt.

The Passover

God said to Moses, "After this plague, Pharaoh will not only let you go, he will throw you out of Egypt altogether. But you must first give him warning of what I mean to do."

So Moses once more stood in front of Pharaoh.

"This is the message from the Lord God of Israel," said Moses. "At midnight all the firstborn children in every family in Egypt shall die. The firstborn animals shall die also. But none of the Israelites shall die in this way."

Pharaoh still would not let the people go.

Moses called together all the leaders of the Israelites. There was a message from God for them too. "You must kill a lamb, a young male that is without blemish. Dip a bunch of herbs into the lamb's blood, and mark your doorposts with it, both sides and at the top. No one must go outside before morning. You shall roast the lamb and eat it with unleavened bread and bitter herbs. And even as you eat, you shall be ready to leave quickly. You must have your shoes on your feet and your staffs in your hands.

"God will pass through the land of Egypt and strike down all the firstborn. But when he sees the blood on your doorposts, he will pass over. Death will not come to your household. You shall remember the passover every year as a covenant between you and God forever."

The people worshiped God. Then they went away to carry out God's instructions.

At midnight every firstborn child in Egypt died, from Pharaoh's own child to the child of the lowliest prisoner in jail. Pharaoh sent for Moses and Aaron.

"Go!" Pharaoh commanded them. "Every one of you can go— even your flocks and herds. Get out from among my people. Go and worship your God."

So the huge host of men, women, and children, with their flocks, their herds, and as many possessions as they could carry, came safely out of Egypt. The Israelites were free.

But their rejoicing did not last long.

The Red Sea

Traveling day and night, the Israelites reached the edge of the wilderness. God led the way in a pillar of cloud by day and a pillar of fire by night. He led them toward the Red Sea by the desert road.

Back in Egypt, Pharaoh and his people realized the Israelites really had gone. Now there were no slaves to do the work. Pharaoh sent his army and six hundred chariots to bring back the Israelites.

The Egyptian army traveled much faster than the Israelites, who had young children and animals with them. The Israelites had almost reached the Red Sea when they looked up and saw the sight they had been dreading. The Egyptians were coming.

"Why did you bring us out here to die?" the people cried to Moses in fear. "It was better to be slaves in Egypt than to die in the wilderness."

"God will fight for you if you will only let him," said Moses.

Then Moses prayed urgently to God.

God answered, "Why are you talking to me? Tell the people to

keep moving forward."

How could they move forward? The sea was in the way!

God was still speaking. "Stretch out your rod over the waters. The sea will divide, and the Israelites will walk across on dry land. The Egyptians will try to follow. Then you and they shall see my power."

Now the pillar of cloud moved from in front of the Israelites to behind them. It came between the Israelites and the Egyptians, bringing darkness to the Egyptian side so that they set up camp for the night. But the cloud brought light to the Israelites on the other side.

Moses told his people to keep moving. Then he stretched out his rod over the sea as God had commanded. The Israelites watched in awe. The waters were dividing.

They started to cross, fearfully at first, then more boldly. All night long the people and animals walked and stumbled across the dry seabed with high walls of water on either side of them.

When the Egyptians realized the Israelites were escaping, they quickly harnessed their horses. They raced their chariots across the ground onto the seabed. They were catching up.

God saw the Egyptians gaining on his people and made the wheels fall off their chariots. The Egyptians struggled in the sand and gasped, "Let's get away from the Israelites. Their God is fighting for them." But they were stuck fast on the seabed, and the last of the Israelites was safely across.

Then God said to Moses, "Stretch out your rod again so that the seas will come together."

In excitement and fear, Moses obeyed. As he held up his rod, the seas came crashing down. Every single one of the Egyptians was drowned; yet every single one of the Israelites was saved, completely unharmed.

Then the Israelites knew their God was great. They sang and danced in triumph and praise.

But once again, their happiness did not last.

In the Wilderness

The Israelites were traveling through the wilderness, hoping to reach the land which God had promised them. But they were becoming desperate.

For three days they had found no water. At last they came to a place called Marah.

"Look!" they cried. "There is water here." They rushed to drink at the pools, but soon they were spitting out the bitter water.

Moses prayed to God. God told him to throw a certain piece of wood into the water. Moses obeyed and the bitter water became sweet and good. Gratefully the Israelites drank their fill.

God made a covenant, an agreement, with them. "If you will keep my laws, I will not send to you any of the plagues which I sent to the Egyptians."

The Israelites traveled on and on. They complained to Moses. "We're hungry. Why didn't you leave us in Egypt? At least we had food there. Why did you bring us out into this desert to starve?"

Then God said to Moses, "I will rain food from heaven for them. They must collect it fresh each morning, and they must collect only enough for one day. I shall test them to see if they are ready to obey my laws. On the sixth day, they may gather enough bread for two days. No one is to go out on the seventh day."

Just before dusk that evening, flocks of small brown birds, quail, came flying low across the ground and landed in the camp. The ground was covered with them. They were very good to eat. Rejoicing, the people collected them. From all over the camp came the smell of roasting. That night the people ate a good meal.

In the morning when the dew had dried up, the ground was covered with tiny white bread-like flakes.

"What is it?" asked the Israelites fearfully. They'd never seen anything like it before.

"This is the food God has sent," Moses explained. "Collect it as he commanded."

So every evening they ate meat, and every morning they ate the bread food, called manna. It was delicious, thin and crisp with a flavor of honey. God told Moses and Aaron to put some of it into a jar to show the future Israelites.

So the Israelites did not starve in the wilderness, but when they came to Rephidim, once more they could not find water.

They shouted at Moses, "Why did you bring us out of Egypt to die of thirst in this place?"

Moses lost patience. "Why are you blaming me? It is really God you're blaming."

Moses said to God, "What am I to do with them? They look angry enough to kill me."

"Walk on in front," said God. "Take some of the leaders with you and carry your rod, the same rod which you had in Egypt. I will meet you by the rock at Horeb. Strike the rock with your rod, and water will flow from it. Then the people may drink."

Moses obeyed. Soon the Israelites were drinking clear, cool water. Would they never stop doubting God and his presence with them?

Exodus 19; 20; 21; 22; 23:1–19; 24:2–8

The Ten Commandments

The Israelites traveled on to the Sinai desert. They camped at the foot of Mount Sinai, and Moses climbed up to the top to speak to God.

God said, "I am going to make a covenant with the Israelites. If you obey my words, you will be my special people, my chosen nation."

Moses excitedly hurried back down the mountain to give the people God's great message.

"Whatever God commands, we will obey," the people promised eagerly.

God was pleased. "On the third day, I will come down to Mount Sinai in a cloud," he told Moses. "The people will see the cloud and know that I am with you. They will trust you. Tell them they must prepare themselves, and you must bless them. During the next two days, they must wash their clothes so that everything is very clean. Also tell them they must not set foot on the mountain, for anyone who even touches it will die. Not until the trumpet sounds may they go up the mountain."

So Moses blessed the people, and they washed their clothes and were very clean. On the morning of the third day, thunder rolled and lightning flashed over the mountain. A thick cloud covered the top of it, and a trumpet sounded loudly. The Israelites shook with fear.

Moses led the people to the foot of the mountain. There they all waited. Then the mountain trembled and the trumpet sounded even louder than before. The mountain was covered with billowing smoke, and God called to Moses.

Moses climbed the mountain and went into the cloud.

God gave Moses the Ten Commandments, saying, "I am the Lord your God who brought you out of Egypt. You must have no gods other than I. You must not worship statues, pictures of images, or anything which you have made yourselves. If you do not obey this

law, I will punish you, your children, and your children's children.

"You must not use the Lord your God's name carelessly or without good reason.

"Remember the Sabbath day and keep it holy. On six days you may work, but on the seventh day, you and all your family must rest.

"Treat your father and your mother with honor and respect.

"Murder no one.

"Do not sleep with another man's wife or another woman's husband.

"Do not steal.

"Do not tell lies or give false evidence against anyone.

"Do not desire for anything which belongs to someone else."

God gave Moses more rules for the Israelites to keep. There were commandments, or rules, about all aspects of life.

Moses wrote down all that God had said and built an altar at the foot of the mountain. And he set up twelve pillars, one for each of the twelve tribes of Israel.

Moses made a sacrifice to God. Then he read the laws to the people and said, "The Lord has made a covenant with you according to all that is written here."

EXODUS 24:12–18; 25; 26; 27; 28; NUMBERS 10:13, 33–36

The Ark of the Covenant

God said to Moses, "Come up to the mountaintop. I will give you tablets of stone on which I have written the commandments."

Moses called to Joshua to come with him. He told the Israelite leaders to wait at the foot of the mountain. "While we are gone, Aaron and Hur will be in charge," he said.

Then Moses and Joshua climbed Mount Sinai. Cloud and fire covered the top of the mountain. For six days Joshua and Moses waited in the cloud. At last God called to Moses. But before God gave Moses the tablets of stone, there was something else God needed to say.

The Israelites were to build an ark, or chest, and a tabernacle, or place of worship. The Ark was to be made of acacia wood. It was to be about forty-five inches long and about twenty-seven inches wide and twenty-seven inches high. It was to be covered with gold inside and out. Four rings were to be made and fastened to its four corners. Two rings would be on one side, two on the other. Poles made of acacia wood and covered with gold were to be slipped through the rings. The poles were never to be taken out of the rings so that the Ark could always be lifted up and carried.

The written laws were to be kept in the Ark, which would be known as the Ark of the Covenant.

God described exactly how the Ark would kept in the Tabernacle. The Tabernacle was to have a curtain hanging in it that would divide the Holy Place from the Most Holy Place. The Ark would be kept in the Most Holy Place.

Then God described what the priests of the Tabernacle should wear. He had even chosen the men who should make all these things.

When God had finished speaking, he gave Moses the two tablets of stone.

The Israelites built the Ark of the Covenant as God had said.

Now it was time to leave Sinai and move on toward the promised land. This time, the Ark of the Covenant was carried in front of them, and the cloud of the Lord was over them.

NUMBERS 13; 14

Twelve Spies Explore Canaan

God spoke to Moses. "Choose twelve men, one from each of the twelve tribes of Israel. They are to go on a secret mission to explore Canaan, the land I have promised to give you."

Moses picked the twelve men carefully, and Joshua was among them. Moses told them exactly what they needed to know about Canaan and its people, if the Israelites were to try an attack.

The twelve men set out. The rest of the Israelites waited as patiently as they could in their camp at Kadesh. For forty days they waited. Then they saw the men returning.

Eagerly the people crowded around, while the twelve men gave a full report on their mission.

"It's a very rich land with good harvests. Look at what we brought back: grapes, figs, and pomegranates. It's a land which flows with milk and honey. But . . ."

The Israelites, who had been getting ready to celebrate, stopped to hear more.

"The cities are large and well-defended," one of the spies said. "And the people are huge, like giants."

The Israelites all began to talk at once.

Caleb, another of the spies, silenced them. "Listen. With God on our side, we can fight and win."

But the other spies spoke so discouragingly that the Israelites were not even willing to try.

The people shouted angrily at Moses and Aaron. "It would have been better if we'd died in Egypt. Why did God bring us here to die in a battle and have our wives and children captured?"

Then everyone wept. Some said, "Let's find another leader, one who will take us back to Egypt."

Joshua stepped forward to stand beside Caleb. The two men tore their clothes as a sign that what they had heard was blasphemy against God.

"The land of Canaan is well worth fighting for," Joshua said. "The Canaanites have no protection against the power of our God."

But the Israelites were too agitated to listen. Some of them picked up stones, ready to throw them at Caleb and Joshua.

In a cloud of glory, God appeared at the Tabernacle so that all the Israelites could see his majesty. He spoke to Moses. "How long will these people refuse to trust me? I will destroy them all."

Moses pleaded with God. Once more God listened to Moses. "Very well, I will forgive them, and they shall live. But not one of the people who were in Egypt shall ever reach the promised land; only their children shall do so. Now turn back into the wilderness. You shall live there for forty years—one year for each day the spies were in Canaan. Of all the men here, only Joshua and Caleb shall reach the promised land."

The Israelites were bitterly sorry for the way they had behaved. For forty long years, they wandered in the desert wilderness.

Moses Dies

"I'm too old now to lead you," Moses told the Israelites. "You must have a new leader."

Moses called Joshua, son of Nun, to come forward. In front of everyone, Moses spoke to him. "Joshua, you must now be the leader. God will be with you. He will never leave you and never forsake you. You must not be afraid."

God himself made a promise to Joshua. "You will bring the Israelites into the land which I have promised them. I myself will be with you."

For the last time, Moses wrote down the laws which God had given to the Israelites, and the book was placed into the Ark of the Covenant. Then Moses wrote a song as God told him to do. It told the story of the past and reminded everyone of the power of God. Moses taught the song to the Israelites so that they would always remember their history.

76

God told Moses to climb Mount Nebo to look across the Jordan River to Canaan spread out below.

"That is the land which I promised to Abraham, Isaac, and Jacob," God said. "I wanted you to see it before you go to your forefathers."

Moses died there on Mount Nebo, and the Lord buried him.

Joshua was the Israelites' new leader, full of strength and wisdom. Moses had blessed him, and the people listened to him.

Joshua told them it was time to prepare to enter the promised land.

Joshua Sends Out Spies

Joshua sent two men on a secret mission to find out how strong the city of Jericho was.

The men entered Jericho openly, pretending to be ordinary visitors. Once inside they looked for somewhere to lodge overnight. The two spies found their way to the house of Rahab. On the way they noted Jericho's strong walls and well-guarded towers.

"It's more of a fortress than a town," they said gloomily.

Rahab let them in. But they had been recognized.

A messenger rushed to tell the king of Jericho. The king, angry and fearful, sent men to capture the spies. It was already dark as the king's men reached Rahab's house. They banged on her front door, shouting, "Bring out the Israelite spies!"

We are trapped! thought the Israelites desperately.

But to their amazement, Rahab lead them up to the roof and hid them under stalks of flax which she had laid out that day to dry.

She then hurried down to open the door for the soldiers.

"It's true that some men did come," she said, "but they left at dusk because they knew the town gates would soon be shut. If you hurry, you can surely catch them."

"They'll have gone toward Jordan," yelled the king's men, and they set off in pursuit.

Up on the roof, the Israelites heard the noise and shouting fade into the distance. They lay still in their hiding place, and presently Rahab crept up to them.

"They've gone," she whispered. "I will tell you why I saved you. We've all heard that your God has given you this land of Canaan. We're afraid because we know how powerful your God is. We heard how he dried up the Red Sea for you. Now I beg you, when you attack the city, please don't harm me, my family, or our possessions."

The spies agreed.

Rahab's house was built on the town wall. She let down a rope from the outside window so that the spies could slide down and get away.

"Go and hide in the mountains for three days," she advised. "The search will be over by then."

And the spies said, "When the Israelites come, you must tie a piece of scarlet cord in this window. Bring your whole family into your house. As long as none of you goes outside, you will not be harmed."

As soon as they had gone, Rahab found a piece of scarlet cord and tied it at the window, taking no chance of being unprepared.

The spies reached the mountains and hid for three days, until the king's men had given up and gone back to the city.

Then the two spies made their way back to Joshua and gave their report. "God has given us the city. All the people of Jericho are terrified of us."

Gratefully Joshua asked God just how the Israelites should occupy the city.

Jericho Falls

Every gate into the city of Jericho was tightly closed and bolted. The people of Jericho knew the Israelites were about to attack, and they were terrified.

But the Israelites were not trained fighters as were the men of Jericho, and the walls of Jericho were very thick and well-fortified.

Then God spoke to Joshua and told him how to capture the city.

Joshua was amazed. For it was indeed a new way to attack a city. But he trusted God, so he gave the orders to the people. And, whatever they thought, the people obeyed.

Every day for six days, they marched around the city of Jericho. The warriors went first. Next came the Ark of the Covenant, carried by the priests. Seven more priests blowing trumpets of rams' horns walked in front of the Ark. Then the rest of the people followed.

"You must be silent, not giving your battle cry until I tell you," Joshua warned the people. So the only sounds were the rams' horns and the tramp, tramp, tramp of marching feet, echoing eerily through the city of Jericho.

On the seventh day, the Israelites got up at dawn and started their march around Jericho. They circled Jericho seven times. On the seventh time, the Israelites completely encircled the city. The priests blew their trumpets, and Joshua yelled, "Shout, for the Lord has given you the city!"

Then the people shouted their battle cry, and the walls of Jericho fell down.

The Israelites swarmed into the city, destroying everyone and everything in it, except the silver and gold and other valuables which Joshua had ordered put into the treasury of the Lord. Joshua forbade the Israelites to keep the gods, or idols, of the people of Jericho, so that the camp of Israel would not be cursed.

Joshua said to the two spies, "Go and bring Rahab and her family out of the city. They can stay with us in our camp."

So Rahab's family was saved, as the men had promised. But the rest of Jericho burned to the ground.

And the Israelites knew that God was with Joshua, as he had been with Moses.

Joshua Conquers Canaan

Jericho had fallen, but the rest of the land of Canaan wasn't yet conquered. Joshua had to decide on the next step in his campaign. He knew that the hard years in the wilderness had made the Israelites stronger. Joshua was sure the Israelites were ready to fight.

But he did not know that one man, Achan, had stolen a bar of gold, some silver, and a beautiful cloak from the treasures of Jericho, and he had buried them under his tent.

Joshua sent men to spy in the city of Ai. "It will be easy," they said when they came back. "You'll need only two or three thousand men. There are hardly any people in Ai."

So Joshua sent three thousand men, but the Israelites were defeated soundly.

Joshua could hardly believe it. He threw himself down on the ground in front of the Ark.

"Lord, why did you bring us to this side of the River Jordan? Everyone will hear about this defeat. They will band together and attack us. We shall all be destroyed. Then who will be left to honor your name?"

God answered, "What are you doing flat on your face? Stand up. One of the Israelites has stolen. The covenant between us is broken. That is why your men were defeated. I was not with you. And I shall not be with you until the man who has stolen is punished."

Then God told Joshua how to reveal the identity of the guilty man.

Joshua called the Israelites together. Grimly he told them what had happened and why they had been defeated. Achan listened, quivering with fear. Joshua went on speaking. The people were to prepare themselves, for tomorrow God would speak. The man who had stolen would be found out.

All night Achan worried. In the morning, Joshua called for the twelve tribes of Israel to come forward, one by one. With God's help, he picked out the tribe of Judah. Achan was one of the tribe of Judah.

From the tribe of Judah, Joshua picked out the clan of the Zerahites. Achan belonged to that clan.

Then Joshua picked out the family of Zimri. Achan was part of that family.

By now Achan was helpless with fear. Sternly Joshua questioned each man in Zimri's family. Achan was discovered, and he was put to death.

Joshua was upset. But God said to him, "Do not be afraid or discouraged. Attack Ai once more. This time I will be with you, and you will triumph."

So Joshua planned carefully and gave orders to his army. Most of them were to hide near Ai while he took a small group of men to make an attack.

As Joshua attacked, all the men of Ai came rushing out, expecting to chase away the Israelites as they had done before. But even as Joshua's army turned and ran, the rest of his army was entering the city, which had been left defenseless.

The men of Ai realized that they had been tricked, and they raced back to save the city, but it was no use. Joshua's group turned and chased them. They were caught between the two parts of Joshua's army, and the men of Ai were defeated.

Joshua built an altar to God and offered a sacrifice of thanksgiving. Then he read the Laws of Moses to the Israelites. The whole nation worshiped God, and God once again blessed them.

Joshua had many more adventures. In the end, he overcame the whole of the land of Canaan.

He divided the land among the twelve tribes of Israel, as God ordered, and for a while there was a rest from war.

The Israelites behaved as usual. Sometimes they remembered God, and things went well for them. But sometimes they forgot God, and disaster followed.

God Chooses Gideon

Joshua had died years before. Now many of the Israelites worshiped false gods, and God had allowed the fierce tribe of the Midianites to overcome Israel.

Gideon was a strong, young Israelite. Yet he had to hide in a winepress as he threshed the wheat that belonged to his family. He was afraid that if he threshed in the open, the Midianites would steal the wheat.

But Gideon was angry as he threshed his wheat. The Israelites were almost starving. Didn't God care? How long would this have to go on? Where was God?

Gideon was startled by a voice. "God is with you, mighty warrior."

Mighty warrior? Him? Gideon turned to look. A man was sitting nearby, watching him. Was the man making fun of him, calling him a mighty warrior when he was hiding in fear? Did he really say God was with Gideon?

Gideon spoke harshly. "God has deserted us. He has simply handed us over to the Midianites."

The man replied, "Go and save Israel. I am sending you."

Then Gideon realized this was no ordinary man. It was an angel with a message from the Lord.

"Me?" asked Gideon. "How can I save Israel? My clan is the weakest in the tribe. And I'm the least important of my family."

God spoke through the angel. "I will be with you. You will be able to defeat the Midianites as if they were just one man."

Gideon tried to understand. "If what you say is true, please give me a sign. Will you wait here a minute?" he begged.

"I will wait," promised the angel.

Gideon rushed away and came back with an offering of meat and bread.

"Put them on that rock," instructed the angel.

Trembling and wondering what would happen, Gideon obeyed.

The angel stretched out the rod he was carrying and touched the food with its tip. Flames of fire instantly sprang up. The food was burned to nothing, and the angel disappeared.

Gideon was terrified. "I have seen the face of the Angel of the Lord," he cried. And he expected to die at once.

God answered, "Don't be afraid. You're not going to die."

That night God told Gideon how to begin the work of saving Israel. He was to destroy the altar to Baal which Gideon's father had set up in the marketplace. Then he was to build a new altar to God.

Gideon swallowed hard. His father and the townspeople would be very angry. They might even kill Gideon. Yet Gideon was ready to obey God.

He thought about it. He didn't dare destroy the altar in daylight, but it might be managed under cover of darkness.

When it was not yet light, Gideon called ten of his servants. They crept down to the marketplace. As quietly as they could, they pulled down the false altar to Baal. In its place they built an altar to God, and Gideon made a sacrifice on it as God had commanded. They then crept home.

When the townspeople saw what had happened, they were furious. "Who did it?" they yelled. They didn't give up their investigations until they discovered it was Gideon, son of Joash.

The townspeople turned on Joash. "Bring out your son! We shall kill him!"

Gideon quivered with fear. Would his father hand him over?

But Joash loved his son dearly. "What?" he said, thinking quickly. "Are you trying to save a god? If Baal really is a god, surely he can defend himself. Let Baal come down and kill my son."

The angry mob listened. If they acted themselves, it would seem as if they thought Baal could do nothing.

"All right," they muttered, "we'll leave it to Baal to punish him."

They waited to see what would happen. Gideon was relieved. He knew Baal had no power at all. And sure enough, he remained completely unharmed. The story soon spread.

When men from all the tribes of Israel heard that Gideon had been chosen by God to be the new leader, they came together to follow him. The sight of so many men ready to trust him almost overwhelmed Gideon. He begged God to send him another sign. God gave him two special signs. Gideon knew that the task of leader really had been given to him and that God would be with him.

He began to think about the task ahead. How could the Midianites be defeated?

JUDGES 7; 8:22–34

Gideon and the Midianites

Gideon had decided on a battle plan. He and his thirty-two thousand men were camped by the well at Harod. The place had been wisely chosen, for the spring which rose there flowed down the hill in a stream, providing plenty of water for an army.

God spoke to Gideon. "You have too many men. If I let you overcome the Midianites with this huge army, the Israelites will say they did it by themselves without my help. Tell anyone who is afraid that he can go home."

Gideon obeyed. The men listened in silence. There was a pause while they looked at each other out of the corners of their eyes. Was anyone going to admit to being afraid?

First one man began to move away, then another, and another, until twenty-two thousand men had left.

Now Gideon understood more of God's meaning. It would have been impossible to control such an enormous number of frightened men in battle. Any victory would have been due to God, but no one would have believed it.

Gideon looked at the men who remained. Ten thousand men of courage would be enough.

But God said, "There are still too many." Still too many? Gideon felt anxious.

"Take the men down to the water to drink," said God. "I will show you which ones to choose."

Puzzled, Gideon ordered his men to go down to the stream. Gideon watched them closely. Most of the men lay on their stomachs to lap water with their tongues. Only three hundred knelt, scooping up the water in one hand.

"Those are the men to choose," said God. Then Gideon realized why. These men were alert, on guard even while they drank. The others had forgotten the enemy in their thirst.

But only three hundred? Against the entire Midianite army?

"With these three hundred, I will give the Midianites into your hands," God promised.

So Gideon told the other men to go back to their tents. But he was very frightened.

God understood. That night he said to Gideon, "Take your servant, Purah, and go under cover of darkness to the Midianite camp. Listen to what they are saying. You will gain courage."

Gideon called to Purah, and together they made their way over the hills to the enemy camp.

At first sight of it in the starlight, Gideon was astounded. The valley was thick with tents. Even the camels were too many to be counted. This army was to be defeated by three hundred men?

Gideon crept down to the edge of the camp. As he sneaked up to listen outside a tent, one of the Midianites inside was telling a dream to a friend.

"I dreamed a loaf of barley bread fell on the camp, and it hit this tent so hard the tent collapsed," he said.

The other Midianite spoke in fear. "The loaf of barley bread stands for the army of Gideon, son of Joash. Their God fights for them. We shall all be destroyed."

The Midianites were in no mood to win a battle. Gideon praised God. Then swiftly he and Purah returned to their own camp.

"Get up!" Gideon shouted to his three hundred men. "We are attacking at once. God will give us the victory."

He divided the men into three groups. To each man he gave a trumpet and an empty jar with a torch inside it. The men looked at Gideon in amazement. What kind of battle was this to be?

"Follow my lead," Gideon ordered. "We will surround the camp in the darkness. When I and my group blow our trumpets, you must blow yours and shout, 'The sword of the Lord and Gideon.'"

The small band of men crept down toward the Midianites. Splitting into three groups, they surrounded the camp.

On the signal from Gideon, they all blew their trumpets and smashed the empty jars. Holding up the torches in their left hands, they yelled their battle cry, "The sword of the Lord and Gideon."

The shouting, the trumpets, the sound of the jars being smashed, and the light of the torches startled the sleeping Midianites. In the darkness, noise, and confusion of the tents, each man believed the other was one of the Israelites. The Midianites began to kill each other. Gideon's astonished army stood firm as the escaping Midianites rushed away from the camp in all directions.

When the light dawned, there were only a small number of men left to fight. Gideon's army was victorious, as God had promised.

The Israelites were delighted and wanted Gideon to rule them.

Gideon refused. "No, God will rule over you." And as long as Gideon was alive, there was peace in the land. The Israelites worshiped the true God.

But Gideon died. And there were more wars and more leaders. The Israelites had many enemies. Among their enemies were the Philistines. Because the Israelites were again doing wrong, God allowed the Philistines to overcome them.

For forty years, the Israelites suffered under the Philistines. But God was about to choose the man who would begin to free them.

Samson and Delilah

Samson was the man chosen by God to help free Israel from the Philistines.

Samson was immensely strong and had a terrible temper. He was always in trouble, either with his own people or with his enemies, the Philistines. For years the Philistines had plotted to capture him, but Samson had always escaped by using the strength which God had given to him.

At last the Philistines realized that the only way they would ever catch Samson would be by trickery. So they watched and waited. One day they learned that he had fallen in love with a woman named Delilah.

The Philistines promised Delilah large sums of money if she could discover what made Samson so strong.

Delilah was no true friend of Samson nor of the Israelites. She was greedy for the money, so she asked Samson about his secret.

"How could anyone possibly tie you up?" she asked, pretending to be playing. For a while, Samson teased her with wrong answers. Each time, Delilah told the Philistines what he'd said. Each time, the Philistines had men hiding in the room, ready to spring out and capture Samson as soon as Delilah had tied him up. But each time, Samson easily broke the bonds before the men had shown themselves.

Delilah kept asking, and finally Samson told her. "My strength lies in my hair, which has never been cut. If my head were shaved, my strength would leave me."

Quickly Delilah sent yet another message to the Philistines. Secretly they came, bringing her promised reward with them. Then while the Philistines hid nearby, Delilah coaxed Samson to sleep with his head lying in her lap. And while he slept, a man cut off all Samson's hair.

Then Delilah cried, "Samson, wake up! The Philistines are upon you!"

Samson jumped to his feet, thinking his strength would save him yet again. But his strength was gone. Then Samson realized that his head had been shaved.

The Philistines blinded him, put him in chains, and took him to the prison. There they set him to heavy work at the grinding mill. Dejected and humbled, Samson struggled with the task.

But while he was in prison, his hair started to grow again.

Some time later, the Philistines held a celebration. It was partly in honor of their god Dagon and partly because they had captured Samson. In the middle of the feast, they called for Samson to be brought to them, so that they could taunt him.

In shuffled the once proud Samson, totally blind, a boy leading him by the hand. Amid the jeers of the crowd, Samson was forced to perform for them. But he managed to whisper to the boy, "Put me near the pillars that hold up this building so that I can lean on them."

The boy did so. Samson could tell that the temple building was crowded with people. More than three thousand men and women were present. Most were on the roof watching Samson. Samson prayed, "God, give me my strength just once more."

He reached toward the two main pillars which held up the temple. He put his right hand on one pillar, and he put his left hand on the other. Then Samson said to God, "Let me die with the Philistines."

With a mighty effort, he pushed the pillars apart. Down crashed the building, killing the rulers and many others. Samson died in the middle of his enemies.

Naomi, Ruth, and Boaz

At the time when the judges were ruling in Israel, there was a famine in the land. Elimelech, who had been born in Bethlehem, took his wife Naomi and his two sons, Mahlon and Chilion, to live in the country of Moab. Elimelech died there, leaving Naomi a widow.

Her sons married two Moabite women, Orpah and Ruth. Later Mahlon and Chilion also died.

When the famine was over, Naomi wanted to return to her own people. So she and her daughters-in-law set out on the journey back to Bethlehem.

Before they had gone far, Naomi stopped. If she took Ruth and Orpah to Bethlehem, they would be far from their own people. Naomi knew how lonely that felt, so she said, "You must each go back to the home of your mother. You've been very good to me, and I hope you'll soon find new husbands in your own land."

The girls looked lovingly at Naomi. "No!" they cried. "We'll come with you."

But in those days a woman without a family to protect her would have a very hard life. Naomi spoke as firmly as she could through her tears. "You must go back."

Weeping bitterly, Orpah kissed Naomi goodbye and started off toward home. But Ruth clung to her mother-in-law.

"Don't ask me to leave you," she sobbed, "nor to return from following after you. For wherever you go, I will go. Where you live, I will live. Your people shall be my people and your God, my God. Wherever you die, I will die and there be buried. Nothing but death shall separate us."

Then Naomi hugged and kissed Ruth, and the two of them went on together.

At last they reached Bethlehem. The people who had known the family years before stared at them. "Is it really you, Naomi?" they asked, hardly recognizing her.

"Don't call me Naomi," she answered. "Call me Mara, 'bitter,' because my husband and sons are dead."

Ruth tried to comfort her mother-in-law. They both felt very lonely. But Naomi did have some relatives in Bethlehem. One of them was a man named Boaz who owned some fields nearby.

It was the time of the barley harvest. Ruth said, "Let me go out to the fields and pick up the grain which the harvesters leave behind on the ground. Then we will be able to make bread and eat."

So with the other people who were too poor to get grain any other way, Ruth went to the fields to glean.

She unknowingly chose to work in the field which belonged to Boaz. It was hard work. Gleaners had to bend low to see the grain, and it could take all day in the hot sun to fill even a small sack.

96

When Ruth had been working for some hours, Boaz came by. He called a greeting to the harvesters. Then he noticed Ruth.

"Who is that girl?" he asked his foreman.

"Her name is Ruth," the man answered. "She came back from Moab with Naomi, your relative. Early this morning she asked if she could glean here. She has hardly stopped to rest all day."

Boaz called to Ruth to come to him. Nervously she approached. Would he send her away?

"Don't go to any other fields. Stay in mine," said Boaz. "And if you are thirsty, drink from my water jars. I'll tell the men not to bother you."

Ruth was very grateful. "Why are you being so kind?" she asked. "I'm a foreigner here."

"I've heard how good you are to Naomi," Boaz answered. "May

God bless you because of it. Come and share our meal with us."

Thankfully Ruth obeyed. She had been feeling very hungry. But as soon as she had eaten enough, she went back to work.

Boaz watched her for a moment. Then he said to his men, "Let her take as much grain as she wants. Drop some on the ground for her."

Ruth gleaned all day. In the evening, she threshed the grain she had gathered and took the barley home to Naomi.

Naomi was amazed. "However did you get this much?" she asked. "Where did you glean?"

"In the field belonging to Boaz," Ruth replied.

"He is one of our close relatives," Naomi answered thoughtfully.

In those days if a man died, it was usual for his brother or closest relative to marry the widow. He would take responsibility for her and for the dead man's land.

Naomi instructed Ruth to make her need for a husband known to Boaz. He was not the family's closest relative, but he wanted to marry her. Before he could do that, he had to settle things with the man who was the closest relative.

Boaz went to the city gate to speak to the man. "Do you want to buy the piece of land which belonged to Elimelech?" he asked. "It is your right as closest relative. If you don't want it, I'll buy it."

"Well, yes, I do want it," said the man.

Boaz had expected this. "If you buy the land, the law is that you must also marry Ruth so that the field stays in Elimelech's family," he said.

The man thought again. "Then I won't buy it," he said. "It would get in the way of the rights of my own children."

So in front of witnesses, Boaz bought the land. Then he and Ruth were married. They had a son called Obed. In time, Obed had a son called Jesse. And Jesse had a son called David. David was to become king of Israel, a great man.

But first, there were many more years while the judges ruled Israel — years during which the boy Samuel was born.

1 SAMUEL 1:1–28; 2:18–21; 3

Samuel in the Temple

There were two Israelite women, Hannah and Peninnah, who were both married to the same man, Elkanah. (It was the custom in those days for a man to have more than one wife.) Peninnah had lots of children, but Hannah had none.

Every year Elkanah and his whole family went to the Temple at Shiloh. There they worshiped God and made a sacrifice to him. Elkanah always gave portions of the meat to Peninnah and her children, but he gave twice as large a portion to Hannah because he loved her very much, knowing how she felt about having no children.

Peninnah also knew, and every year she made things much worse for Hannah by teasing her cruelly.

"What's wrong?" Elkanah asked tenderly. "Am I not worth more to you than ten children?"

But Hannah wept and refused food. Later when she went to the Temple, she prayed desperately to God. "Lord, if you will only let me have a baby son, I promise I will give him back to you. He shall serve you all his life."

Eli the priest noticed her. When he heard her story, he spoke kindly. "Peace be to you. May the Lord God give you what you ask."

Hannah felt better. She even felt hungry enough to eat some food.

The family returned home to Ramah, and before too long, Hannah did indeed have a baby boy. She was overjoyed and named him Samuel. She loved him very much, but she hadn't forgotten her promise to God.

That year when Elkanah and the family went to Shiloh, Hannah and the baby stayed home.

"He's too young to leave me yet," she said, cradling Samuel in her arms.

"Do whatever you think is best," Elkanah answered gently.

Another year went by. Hannah watched her baby growing bigger. Soon he was able to walk, able to run, beginning to talk. Sometimes her heart ached, but she never faltered in her resolve.

Finally, when the child had been weaned, Hannah knew it was time to complete her promise. That year when it was the time for sacrifice, Hannah and Samuel went to the Temple at Shiloh with the others.

Elkanah made the sacrifice. Then with a pounding heart, Hannah carried her tiny boy over to where Eli the priest stood. Elkanah was beside her, but it was Hannah who spoke.

"Do you remember me?" she asked Eli. "I'm the woman who prayed so hard for a child. This is the boy God gave to us. Now I give him back to God."

So Hannah left Samuel with Eli the priest to grow up in the Temple, and she and Elkanah returned to Ramah.

At first they missed Samuel very much, but they saw him every year when they made their visit to Shiloh. Hannah always took new clothes for him, and Eli always blessed Hannah and Elkanah, asking God to send them more children. Before long, Hannah had three more boys and two girls, so she was happy.

Eli was very glad to have Samuel. His own two sons were wicked and no comfort to him.

As Samuel grew up, he listened as Eli taught him about God, and he helped more and more in the work of the Temple.

One night the boy was lying on his bed in the Temple near the Ark of the Covenant when he heard a voice call his name.

"Samuel."

Samuel had been almost asleep. Now he quickly awoke. He sat up. Who had spoken? In the dim light of the lamp which was always kept burning, he looked around.

There was no one to be seen. It must have been Eli calling him. Eli was old now and almost blind. Maybe something was wrong. Samuel sprang up and ran to Eli's bedside. "Here I am," he panted. "You called me."

Eli was puzzled. "I didn't call you," he said. "Go back to bed."

Perhaps he had been dreaming. Samuel went back and lay down.

"Samuel."

The voice called again. Samuel scrambled to his feet and ran in to Eli. "Here I am. You did call me," he said.

"No," said Eli, still not properly awake. "I didn't call you. Go and lie down."

Slowly Samuel made his way back and lay down. He was wide awake. He lay there in the near darkness, and the voice called again.

"Samuel."

Samuel got up slowly. Slowly he went to Eli. Taking a deep breath, he said, "Here I am. You did call me."

Now Eli was fully awake too. He realized what was happening. God himself was calling Samuel.

"Go and lie down," Eli said gently. "And if you hear the voice again, say, 'Speak, Lord. Your servant is listening.'"

Once more Samuel lay down in the Temple near the Ark of the Covenant.

Half excited and half afraid, he waited. Again God spoke. "Samuel."

Samuel found his voice. "Speak, Lord. Your servant is listening," he said.

Then God gave Samuel a message for Eli. It was such a sad message that as Samuel listened, he wanted to cry. He didn't go rushing in to tell Eli. He lay still.

In the morning he got up and started to work, trying to keep out of Eli's way. But Eli called him over. "Samuel, my son, what did God say to you?"

Then Eli saw the look on the boy's face. "Don't be afraid to tell me," he said gently.

So Samuel repeated the message. Eli's family was to be punished because of the wickedness of Eli's two sons.

"God knows best," Eli answered quietly. "Let him do whatever seems right to him."

As Samuel grew older, all the Israelites knew that God was with him, and they listened to his words.

But before long the punishment of Eli's family and the Israelites was to begin.

The Philistines and the Ark of the Covenant

The Israelites were again fighting with the Philistines, but this time, because of the wickedness of the Israelites, God allowed the Philistines to overcome them.

"Let us take the Ark of the Covenant into battle with us," cried the leaders of the Israelites when their defeated army came straggling back. "The Ark will give us victory."

So some men went to Shiloh to get the Ark, and Eli's two sons were among the priests who came back with it.

When the weary Israelites saw the Ark of the Covenant being carried into their camp, they gave a great shout of gladness.

Over in their own camp, the Philistines heard it. What's going on over there? they wondered. A defeated army did not usually shout in triumph.

The Philistines sent spies out. Later the spies came back saying, "A god has come into the camp of the Israelites."

Then the Philistines were even more afraid. They said, "We must fight harder or the Israelites will make us their slaves."

So the Philistines attacked with all their might. Thousands of Israelites were killed, including Eli's sons. Worst of all, the Ark of the Covenant was captured by the Philistine army.

A messenger ran from the battlefield to Shiloh. His clothes were torn and dust was on his head. As soon as the townspeople saw him, they guessed the battle was lost. When they heard the whole truth, there was a tremendous outcry from the heartbroken Israelites.

Eli was blind now. He sat anxiously on a seat by the side of the road, waiting for news of his sons. When he heard the cries of the people, he asked desperately, "What is it? What's happening?"

The messenger hurried over to the old man. "I've just come from the battlefield," he said. "Israel was defeated. Your sons are dead. And the Ark of the Covenant has been captured."

With the news of the Ark, Eli fell back off his seat and died of a broken neck.

The triumphant Philistines had carried the Ark into the temple of their god Dagon in Ashdod. But when they came back in the morning, Dagon had fallen flat on his face in front of the Ark.

The Philistines stood him up again. But the next morning, not only was Dagon lying flat on the ground, but his head and his hands were broken off as well. The people of Ashdod became afflicted with tumors, and they begged their rulers to take the Ark away.

The Ark was moved to Gath. The people of Gath became ill. They were terrified and sent the Ark to Ekron. But when the people of Ekron saw it being brought into the city, they called out, "Don't bring it here or we shall all die! Send it back to the Israelites."

The frightened Philistines asked their priests how they should return the Ark. "You must send it with an offering to show you are sorry," the priest replied. So the Philistines placed the Ark in a cart, with images of golden rats and golden tumors in a chest beside it. They harnessed the cart to two milk cows and set it off along the road

toward Beth Shemesh where the Israelites were.

The people of Beth Shemesh were harvesting in their fields.
When they saw the driverless cart coming down the road, they
realized the Ark of the Covenant was inside. As they watched,
spellbound, the cart stopped beside the field of Joshua. The Israelites
ran to it and lifted out the Ark with great rejoicing.

When the watching Philistines saw that the Ark had been safely
returned, they went back to Ekron, breathing sighs of relief.

The Israelites sacrificed the two milk cows to God. When Samuel
heard the news of the Ark's return, he said, "If you are really ready to
serve the Lord God, destroy all your false gods."

The Israelites obeyed. Before long the Philistine army again
attacked. But now God was on the side of the Israelites. The
Philistines were soundly defeated.

For many years there was peace in the country, but then the
Israelites grew restless.

The Israelites Demand a King

Samuel was growing old. He was too old to go on ruling over the Israelites, so he appointed his two sons in his place. But his sons were unjust and took bribes.

The people complained. "We want a king to rule over us," they declared. Samuel was distressed. He prayed to God about it.

"Tell them," said God, "if they do have a king, he will treat them harshly. They will cry to me for help, and I will not listen to their cries."

Samuel gave God's message to the people, but they paid no attention. "We want a king," they repeated stubbornly. "Besides, if we have a king, we shall be like all the other nations."

Samuel told God what the people said.

"Very well," said God. "We shall give them a king."

1 SAMUEL 9; 10; 11:15; 12:24–25

Saul Becomes King

Saul was a young Israelite of the tribe of Benjamin. One day his father, Kish, said to Saul, "Our donkeys have strayed. Take one of the servants and go look for them."

Saul obeyed. He and the servant walked many miles, searching for the animals without success. After three days Saul said wearily, "Let's go back, or my father will be more worried about us than he is about the donkeys."

"Wait," said the servant. "I've heard of a holy man who lives in a town near here. Let's see if he can tell us which way to go."

"All right," said Saul. So they set off to find Samuel, the holy man.

Only the day before, God had said to Samuel, "The man whom you must anoint king of Israel will come to you tomorrow. He will be from the tribe of Benjamin."

Now Samuel stood at the gateway of the town. As soon as he caught sight of Saul coming toward him, God said to Samuel, "This is the man."

Saul unsuspectingly walked straight up to Samuel. "Will you tell me how to get to the house of the holy man?"

Samuel answered quietly, "I am the man for whom you are looking. Come and have a meal with me. Don't worry any more about the lost donkeys. They have been found."

While Saul still gazed at him in astonishment, Samuel said, "You are the man the people of Israel have been wanting."

"What?" responded Saul. "But I come from the smallest tribe in Israel. And my family is of no importance even in our small tribe."

"Come," said Samuel. Saul and his servant went with Samuel. They shared a meal with about thirty people, and Samuel ordered that Saul be given a special portion of meat. Afterward Samuel took Saul up to the roof of his house. They sat in the cool light of the stars and talked. When Saul grew sleepy, Samuel gave him a bed on the roof.

The next morning Saul awoke refreshed. Then he and his servant set out for home. At the edge of town, the servant was sent on ahead while Samuel quietly anointed Saul's head with oil in the ceremony that was to be used to anoint Israel's kings throughout the years. Samuel told Saul of signs by which Saul could know he really was the man chosen by God to be king of Israel.

Saul set off along the road with his thoughts whirling. By the time he reached home, God had spoken to him through several signs. Saul's behavior was so different that his family wondered what had happened to him. But Saul did not yet tell them of his encounter with Samuel.

Then Samuel called the Israelites together. "You wanted a king," Samuel said. "Now God will show you who it is to be."

One by one, all the tribes of Israel came forward, but Samuel sent each tribe back until the tribe of Benjamin approached him. After choosing the tribe of Benjamin, Samuel saw each family in the tribe and chose the family of Kish. Finally Saul was chosen, but he was nowhere to be found.

The people asked God, "Where is Saul?"

"He's hiding among your possessions," answered God.

Then the people ran and found Saul, and they brought him out. As Saul stood in front of them, he was unsure whether to be proud or embarrassed, because he was much taller than anyone else there.

"See the man whom God has chosen," announced Samuel. "There is no one like him."

"Long live the king," shouted the Israelites.

Then Samuel explained to the people exactly what the powers of a king were and told them the rules that would be kept. Then he wrote everything down, so that there might be no misunderstanding.

So Saul became king and began his rule over the Israelites. Samuel warned the people, "Remember the great things God has done for you. Love and serve God faithfully. For if you keep doing wrong, you and your kind will be overcome by your enemies."

1 SAMUEL 13:1, 11–14; 16:1–13

David, Jesse's Son

At first Saul ruled well and kept God's laws. He had a son, Jonathan, whom he loved dearly.

But after some years, Saul grew proud. He began to do as he wanted and then made excuses to Samuel.

"Your kingdom won't last," Samuel warned him sadly, "because you keep disobeying God."

Finally God said to Samuel, "How much more time are you going to waste being sad about Saul? I no longer want him to be king. Go to Bethlehem to the house of a man called Jesse. I've chosen one of his sons to be the next king. You must go and anoint the boy."

"If Saul discovers why I've gone, he'll kill me," protested Samuel.

God said, "Go to Bethlehem, but take a calf with you. Tell the people there that you have come to make a sacrifice."

Samuel loved and trusted God, so he took the calf as God had commanded. When he reached Bethlehem, the leaders of the city came out to meet him with fear on their faces.

"Why have you come?" they asked nervously.

"I have come in peace," Samuel reassured them. "I'm going to offer a sacrifice to God here." Then he sent a message to Jesse, asking him to bring his sons to the sacrifice.

Jesse and seven of his sons hurried to wash themselves and put on clean clothes, as was the custom before making a sacrifice. Then they came to Samuel.

One at a time, Jesse ordered his sons to stand in front of the holy man. When Samuel saw Eliab, the eldest, he thought this must be the one, for Eliab was very handsome.

"No," said God. "You are looking only at the outside of a person. I look at his heart. What a person believes, how he feels, and the way he acts are more important than the way he looks. I have not chosen

Eliab to be the next king."

The next son stood in front of Samuel, and the next, until all seven had stood there. But still God made no sign.

Samuel was puzzled. Then he had an idea. "Have you any more sons?" he asked.

Jesse stared at Samuel in surprise.

"Only David," he replied. "He's the youngest. He's out looking after the sheep."

"Send for him," Samuel ordered. Soon David arrived, flushed and panting. He was handsome, and his eyes were full of courage.

"This is the one," God said to Samuel. "Anoint his head with oil."

Samuel obeyed. David's father and brothers watched in amazement. Did this mean David was to be a follower of Samuel?

Samuel did not explain. David went back to tending the sheep. But from that day, the Spirit of the Lord was with him.

Soon God's plan for David began to take shape.

David Meets Saul

The Spirit of the Lord was no longer with Saul. Instead, he felt tormented, utterly sad, and hopeless. At times he felt angry and even violent.

Saul's servants noticed that music could soothe him and would often cure him for a while.

"Sir," they said, "why not appoint a musician to your court? Then he could play for you whenever the distressing spirit comes upon you."

"Find a musician then," Saul ordered. "But he must play well."

One of the servants said to Saul, "Sir, I know of a musician. He sings his own songs and plays the harp as well. He plays extremely well. He is a brave young man who would make an excellent warrior. His name is David. He is a son of Jesse of Bethlehem, and the Spirit of the Lord is with him."

"Send for him," commanded Saul.

Messengers rushed to Bethlehem to find David and his father, Jesse.

"King Saul wants to see your son David," they told Jesse.

Jesse agreed to send his son to see Saul, but he was puzzled by this new interest in his youngest son.

Once more David was called in from tending the sheep. Hurriedly he was told the news, and almost before he could take it in, David found himself being hustled into clean clothes for the journey. Jesse rushed about to find some gifts David could take to the king.

Soon David set off with the messengers. He carried with him gifts for King Saul: a donkey loaded with bread, a skinful of wine, and a young goat.

"Where's your harp?" asked the messenger. "Don't forget to bring that with you."

"I have it here," said David. He always had his harp with him.

When they arrived at the court, David was taken to the king. Saul liked the look of him at once. "You shall be an armorbearer," Saul announced. And he sent a messenger to Jesse, asking that David be allowed to stay for a while.

After that, David lived partly with Saul's men and partly at home, caring for the sheep.

But whenever the distressing spirit came upon Saul, a messenger was sent for David. And David hurried to court and played his harp until the beautiful sounds calmed Saul's tormented mind.

But trouble was coming for the Israelites.

David and Goliath

The army of the Philistines marched into the land of the Israelites, intending to occupy it. King Saul gathered his army to repel the Philistines, and the two armies set up camp on either side of a valley. Neither army wished to start the battle, because whoever attacked first would have to fight uphill. The soldiers would be an easy target for the spears and arrows which the enemy would hurl down.

It seemed as if the armies would be there forever. Then one day, out from the Philistine camp marched Goliath, an enormous man over nine feet tall. He was protected by heavy armor and carried a huge spear. He bellowed a challenge across the valley to King Saul's army.

"If any man can defeat me single-handedly, we will be your slaves. But if I defeat him, you Israelites will be our slaves."

His voice echoed around the mountains. Instead of taking up his challenge, King Saul's men turned away in fear.

King Saul offered a reward of immense riches and marriage to his daughter to the man who would fight Goliath. But no one volunteered. Every day Goliath hurled his challenge across the valley. Every day Saul's men cowered in a silence of fear and anger.

Three of David's older brothers were in Saul's army. David was looking after the sheep at home when his father, Jesse, called to him. "I want you to go and see how your brothers are doing," he said. "Bring me word from them."

Gladly David set out. It was a half-day's walk, but he kept going until at last he could see the tents of King Saul's army.

Just as he reached the camp, the army was ordered to go to their battle positions. Eagerly, David ran to find his brothers.

Before he could do more than greet them, Goliath marched out from the camp of the Philistine army and yelled his challenge.

David waited, expecting someone to spring forward in reply. Instead the Israelites turned away.

David couldn't believe his ears and eyes. "Who is this man who challenges the army of God's people?" he asked. "If no one else will fight him, I will!"

"You?" jeered his brothers. "You only came to watch the battle. Go home and look after the sheep."

David flushed angrily, but he had learned self-control. He answered quietly, "Can't I even speak?"

He talked to more of the soldiers, and some of them went to tell the king what David was saying.

Saul sent for David. Soon David stood in front of the king. David's heart beat quickly, but he spoke steadily.

"No one needs to be afraid of Goliath. I will fight him."

"You?" responded Saul. "You're only a youth. He's a trained fighting man."

"I am a shepherd," David answered. "When a bear came to carry off a lamb, I killed it. Another time I had to kill a lion. God saved me from the lion and the bear, and God will save me from this Philistine."

So King Saul said, "Very well. Go, and the Lord be with you." The king put his own armor on David and gave him a sword.

Clank, clank, David tried to walk. He could hardly move. The armor was too heavy, and David had not been trained to fight with a sword. He struggled out of the armor and put on his own shepherd's tunic. Then he took his rod and his shepherd's sling, the sling from which he'd often thrown stones to drive wild animals away from the sheep. David went out to face Goliath.

A silence fell over the whole valley. David's brothers watched, hardly daring to breathe.

Calmly David walked down to the little stream which flowed through the valley. Bending down, he carefully picked out five smooth, round stones from the water's edge. Then he stood up and spoke clearly. "I am ready," he said.

Goliath stepped forward and saw David. "You're just a boy! You dare to challenge me? I'll cut you into pieces and give you to the birds and beasts to eat."

David replied steadily, "I come in the name of God. He is with me. I will kill you, Goliath, and everyone will know that the God of the Israelites is the one true God."

Furious, Goliath moved forward to attack. But David rushed ahead and placed one of the stones in his sling. Then he whirled the sling around.

The stone flew straight as an arrow, striking Goliath's forehead with full force. Down fell the giant, flat on the ground. David ran forward, took Goliath's own sword, and cut off the giant's head.

When the Philistines saw that their champion was dead, they turned and ran. With a great shout, King Saul's army pursued them. The Philistines were defeated and chased out of the country.

On that day King Saul took David in, and he lived with the king. For a while David was happy in the palace, but more trouble was coming.

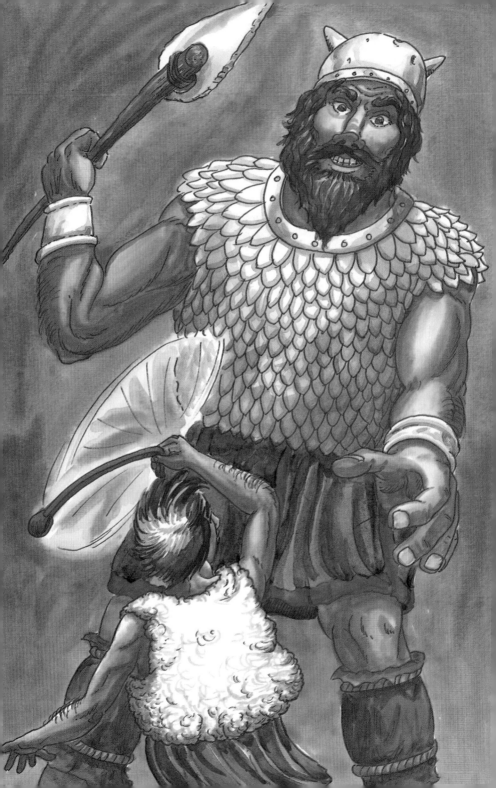

1 Samuel 18; 19:1–17

David and Saul

David's life had changed completely. He was treated as if he were King Saul's own son. And Saul's son Jonathan, far from being jealous, became David's greatest friend.

Whatever Saul asked David to do, David did well. Whenever David led his men in battle against the Philistines, the Israelites won. At first Saul was pleased. But soon he noticed how popular David was becoming. The Israelite women sang a song: "Saul has killed thousands in his battles, but David had killed tens of thousands."

When Saul heard those words, he fumed, "I suppose soon he'll be wanting my kingdom."

The next day the distressing spirit came upon Saul. As always, he sent for David, who played his harp in an attempt to soothe Saul. Saul sat watching the boy while dark and angry thoughts grew in his mind.

Saul remembered how everyone had praised David. Perhaps David really might be the man God had chosen to be king in Saul's place. The thought was too much. Without warning, Saul sprang up and hurled a spear at David, meaning to pin him to the wall.

Although David was taken completely by surprise, he was too quick for Saul. David leaped to one side. Twice Saul hurled a spear. Twice David escaped by leaping aside. David stood panting and watchful, ready to dodge yet again.

But Saul realized he could never harm David that way. He would need a plan. Saul ordered David to leave.

Later Saul made David captain over a thousand soldiers, thinking that when David next led the soldiers into battle, he would be killed. But David was not killed. He fought bravely and won many honors, because God was with him. David behaved so wisely and so well that the people loved and praised him more than ever.

Saul pretended to be friendly toward David, but inwardly his hatred grew. Then his daughter Michal fell in love with David.

"I can use her love as a trap," schemed Saul. He sent servants with a message to David. "The king is pleased that his daughter loves you," said the servants. "You can marry her and become his son-in-law."

"But I'm a poor man," replied David. "I can't marry a princess."

Secretly delighted to hear that David had answered as expected, Saul sent another message. "The king says you may marry the princess if you will pay the price."

"What price?" asked David, puzzled. Saul knew he had no riches.

You must provide proof that one hundred of the king's enemy, the Philistines, have been killed," said the servant.

"I accept," said David. Saul was overjoyed. Surely David would be killed now in trying to kill one hundred men.

But David killed not only the hundred Philistines that Saul required, but two hundred. Inwardly raging, Saul was forced to honor his promise, and David married Saul's daughter Michal.

Saul made plan after plan to trap David, but each time David escaped unharmed, once with the help of his wife, Michal.

Saul could hide his anger no longer. He went to Jonathan and his servants. "Catch David and kill him," he ordered.

119

But Jonathan was David's friend and would never harm him. Slipping away from the camp, Jonathan hurried to warn David.

"My father wants to kill you. Tonight you must go into hiding. I'll speak to my father about you, and I'll warn you when he is about to move against you."

So David hid. The next morning Jonathan went to Saul and asked, "Why do you want to harm David? He has served you faithfully."

As Jonathan pleaded, Saul listened, and his anger melted away. Saul made a promise. "As surely as our God is alive, David will not be killed by me," he said.

Gladly Jonathan ran to tell David and bring him back to Saul. For a short time, the friends were as happy as before. But soon war broke out anew. David fought as bravely as ever, the people shouted his praises, and Saul felt the old hatred return.

Saul was again troubled by a dark spirit. Remembering that his music had often calmed the king, David took his harp and began to play. But this time music did not help. Saul seized a spear and once again tried to pin David to the wall. As before, David was able to avoid Saul. Overcome with his rage, Saul drove the spear deep into the wall.

David knew he must get away.

120

1 SAMUEL 20; 31; 2 SAMUEL 1:1–10, 17–27; 5:1–3; 9

David and Jonathan

David began running from King Saul, with the king's men chasing him from place to place. After many months, David grew tired and weary. He needed to talk to Jonathan.

"Why is your father trying to have me killed?" he asked.

"He's not," said Jonathan. "He promised."

But David was so certain that Jonathan agreed to do whatever his friend thought best.

The next day was a special festival, and David was to dine with the king. Instead, David planned to hide in a field nearby. Jonathan, however, would dine with Saul. If the king grew very angry because David was missing, Jonathan would know that Saul was plotting David's death.

David and Jonathan agreed on a secret signal so that David would know if it was safe to return or if he should escape quickly.

So it was arranged. While Jonathan dined with the king, Saul asked where David was. As Jonathan spoke about David, Saul became so angry that he hurled a spear at Jonathan.

Jonathan knew that David was right. Sadly he sent the secret message to David. David must go at once.

As long as Saul lived, he made no peace with David. Twice David had Saul at his mercy, yet spared his life.

Finally Saul fought his last battle with the Philistines. Jonathan and Saul's two other sons were killed in the battle, and Saul was badly wounded. Rather than allow the Philistines to kill him, Saul took his own sword and fell on it. As he was dying, he asked an Amalekite to give him the final blow.

When David heard the news, he mourned bitterly for his friend Jonathan. He was also sad about Saul.

In due time, David was made king of Israel in Saul's place. One of his first tasks was to capture Jerusalem from the Jebusites. He made it the capital city of Israel, and it was called "The City of David." He brought the Ark of the Covenant to Jerusalem. David wanted to build a temple in which to keep the Ark, but God said, "No, but one of David's sons shall build the Temple in Jerusalem."

All this time David had not forgotten his friend Jonathan. "Are none of his family left alive?" David asked.

"Jonathan's son still lives," his servants answered. "He is named Mephibosheth, and he is a cripple. He cannot walk properly."

David sent for Mephibosheth and, for Jonathan's sake, gave back to him all the land which had belonged to Saul. Mephibosheth lived at the palace with David and was treated kindly.

After many years, David was old and knew he was about to die. He sent for his son Solomon.

"I am going the way of all flesh on earth," said David. "You must be strong. Do as the Lord says. Walk in his ways. Lead the people of Israel to do right in his eyes. Then the Lord will keep his promises to Israel. Be wise, my son, and show yourself to be a man."

David gave a few more instructions to Solomon. Then, wearily, he lay back on his pillows and fell asleep. And in his sleep, he died.

During David's long life, he wrote many songs. Some of David's songs, called psalms, are still sung today. They are contained in the Book of Psalms.

A Psalm of David

The Lord is my shepherd; I shall not want.
He makes me to lie down in green pastures;
    he leads me beside the still waters.
He restores my soul; he leads me in the paths of
    righteousness for his name's sake.
Yea, though I walk through the valley of the shadow
    of death, I will fear no evil, for you are with me;
    your rod and your staff, they comfort me.
You prepare a table before me in the presence of my
    enemies; you anoint my head with oil; my cup runs over.
Surely goodness and mercy shall follow me all the days
    of my life; and I will dwell in the house of the Lord forever.

1 KINGS 3; 4:34; 5:4–5

Solomon's Wisdom

After David died, Solomon became the ruler of thousands of
Israelites. He felt he could never cope with his new position. People
kept bringing problems to him which he was expected to solve. And
his father, David, was not there to advise him.

Solomon tried to follow his father's instructions and keep God's
laws. His people were still making sacrifices in many places of
worship because there was no temple.

One day Solomon himself went to Gibeon to offer a sacrifice.
That night as he lay sleeping, God came to him in a dream.
"Solomon," said God, "what gift would you like to have from me?"

"Oh," said Solomon, "give me wisdom. I am so young, and I
don't know how to rule your people wisely."

God was pleased. "Because you have asked for wisdom, I will
give it to you. You shall be wiser than anyone ever was. No one shall
ever be as wise as you again. And I will give you the honor and
wealth which you did not ask for. If you keep my laws, I will give
you a long life as well."

Solomon woke up and opened his eyes. Had it just been a dream?

In the morning Solomon went to Jerusalem to offer a sacrifice.
Then he held a great feast for his court.

Two women asked for an audience with him. One of them carried
a baby in her arms.

"My Lord Solomon," pleaded the other woman, "this woman and
I share a house. I had a baby. Three days later, she had a baby. During
the night, her baby died. There was no one else in the house, and I
was asleep. She took my baby and put her dead baby beside me.
When I woke up, I started to feed my son and saw that he was dead. I
cried and cried. But when the morning light came, I looked at him,
and I could see it wasn't my baby at all. She had my baby."

"No," cried the second woman, hugging the baby to her. "She's lying. Her baby died. This one is mine."

"One of you is lying," said Solomon. "Bring a sword," he ordered. Everyone watched in silence as a soldier brought the sword.

"Now," said Solomon, "the child shall be cut in half. You can each have half."

"No!" screamed the first woman. "That would kill the baby!"

But the second woman nodded. "It is fair. Neither of us should have him. Divide him in two." The soldier lifted the sword.

Sobbing, the first woman pleaded with the king. "No, no, give the baby to her. Don't kill him!"

Solomon spoke. "Give the baby to the first woman. She is his real mother. It is obvious who truly loves the child."

Because of this, all the people marveled at Solomon's wisdom.

Solomon continued to give wise judgments. In only four years as king, he became rich and powerful as God had promised. People of all nations came to listen to him and ask for help with their own problems. Each one brought gifts.

Solomon wanted to show his love for God. It was time to start building the Temple where God could be worshiped, where the Ark of the Covenant could be kept in safety and with honor.

1 Kings 6; 7:13–22, 51; 8:1–7
Building the Temple

The work of building the Temple began. Solomon wanted only the most skilled craftsmen to work on it and only the finest of materials to be used. To search for these, he sent messengers to all parts of Israel and beyond.

Materials began to arrive. Sweet-smelling cedar wood from Lebanon was used for the walls and ceilings. Pine trees were sawed into planks for the floors. All the stone was cut and shaped in the quarries, so that no sound of iron tools should disturb the peace of the Temple Courts, even while they were being built.

The Temple was about ninety feet long, thirty feet wide, and over forty-five feet high. It was three stories high. It had an inner room, called the Holy of Holies, or Most Holy Place. In the inner room was the altar where the Ark of the Covenant would be placed.

Two cherubim were carved from olive wood and overlaid with gold. They were placed so that their wings would be outstretched over the Ark. All the walls were beautifully carved. The altar was made from cedar wood overlaid with gold. By the time the Temple was finished, all the inside surfaces were overlaid with pure gold.

Solomon went to Tyre to see a man called Huram. Huram was especially skilled at working in bronze. Solomon gave him instructions, and Huram built two huge columns of bronze to stand at the entrance to the Temple. Each was about twenty-seven feet high and beautifully carved. The columns were given names. The one on the south side was called Jachin, which means "he (God) establishes," and the one on the north side was called Boaz, which means "in him (God) is strength."

For seven years the building of the Temple continued. At last it was finished. The Temple had been built to the glory of God, and it was very beautiful

Solomon brought all the treasures which had belonged to King

David and placed them in the Temple. Then, offering sacrifices, the priests lifted up the Ark of the Covenant on its two poles and carried it to the place prepared for it in the Holy of Holies.

All the people rejoiced and were glad. But Solomon's reign was not over.

The Queen of Sheba

Solomon built a large navy with ships which sailed to many ports, and so his fame spread. News of his wisdom reached the court of the Queen of Sheba. For a while she listened to the tales told about King Solomon. Then she declared, "Nonsense, no man could be so wise."

"Indeed, the stories are true," her attendants persisted.

"I shall go and see for myself," announced the queen. She traveled across the desert with a great number of servants and brought many splendid gifts of gold, precious stones, and silks.

The arrival in Jerusalem of the Queen of Sheba was magnificent. Solomon, dressed in his most beautiful robes, sat on his throne awaiting her. In she swept, wearing silks and linens, splendid with pearls and rubies. A long line of slaves carrying gifts followed her.

The two rulers greeted each other. Then the queen began to test Solomon, asking him many questions to judge his wisdom.

But Solomon answered every one of her questions wisely.

A great feast was held for the queen. Afterwards Solomon took her to the entrance of the Temple. She looked at its magnificence and cried, "Everything I heard about you is true. Blessed be the Lord your God who has shown you such favor. Surely God must love Israel very much to give it a king such as you."

She gave Solomon many gifts, and in exchange he gave her anything she asked for. It was a splendid and satisfying visit.

The Queen of Sheba and her servants returned to their home, but Solomon's wealth continued to grow. As more people heard of the wisdom which God had given him, many came to ask him questions, each one bringing gifts. Solomon's army grew to twelve thousand horsemen and one thousand four hundred chariots. In Jerusalem, he made silver as plentiful as stones.

Through the gift of wisdom, God had made Solomon a very great king. But perhaps Solomon had become too great.

Solomon's Reign Ends

Solomon became very proud. He did not remain loyal to God, and he began to worship false gods.

God was very angry. "For as long as you live, I will keep my promise," God said to him. "Israel shall remain one nation. But when you die, the people shall divide into two nations, and the two tribes of the south shall be at war with the ten tribes of the north."

For forty years Solomon reigned over Israel, and it did remain one nation. Then Solomon died.

Elijah, the Ravens, and the Widow

Now Israel was divided into two kingdoms. Both were ruled by wicked kings, but Ahab, king of the ten tribes of the north, was the worst. Most of the people in Ahab's kingdom forgot about God and began to worship Baal.

But one man, Elijah, remained faithful, and God gave him a message for Ahab.

Bravely Elijah stood in front of the king. "I am the prophet of the true God," said Elijah. "And I tell you that unless I say so, there will be no rain or dew in this country for the next few years." Then he rushed hastily from the palace before Ahab could have him arrested.

"Go and hide by the brook Cherith near the River Jordan," God commanded. "I will send ravens to feed you there, and you will be able to drink from the brook."

Elijah hurried to the hiding place. But he wondered how ravens could feed him. Was he to catch and kill them?

That evening the ravens came, carrying bread and meat in their beaks. The birds dropped the food and Elijah ate. Every morning and evening for as long as Elijah hid there, the ravens came with food.

After a while, the brook dried up because there had been no rain. Now what? thought Elijah. I shall die of thirst.

But God had a plan. "Go to Zarephath. I have ordered a widow who lives there to feed you."

Elijah set off for Zarephath. As he reached the gates of the town, he saw a widow gathering sticks for a fire. Thirsty and hungry, Elijah spoke. "Please, will you bring me some water so that I may drink?"

The widow turned at once to bring it. Elijah called after her, "And please, will you bring me a small piece of bread?"

She paused anxiously. "Truly, I have no bread. All I have left is one handful of flour and a little oil. I'm gathering these sticks so that I can cook one last meal for myself and my son. After that, we shall starve to death."

"Cook your meal," said Elijah, "but first make me a little cake. Afterward make some for yourself and your son, for the Lord God of Israel promises that your bin of flour shall not be empty, nor shall the jar of oil, until the day when he shall send rain on the land again."

The widow obeyed. And sure enough, each time she took flour from the bin, there was just as much left. So it was with the oil as well. She, her household, and Elijah had food for many days.

After Elijah had lived in the house for a while, the widow's son became ill and stopped breathing. The widow cried out to Elijah, "Did you come here to show me I had done wrong and to kill my son?"

"Give the boy to me," Elijah answered. He carried the boy up to the room where he was staying and prayed desperately. Then Elijah laid the boy on the bed. He stretched himself over the boy three times. God heard Elijah's cry for help, and the boy began to breathe.

Elijah carried him downstairs where the mother sat weeping. He gently placed the boy in her arms. For a moment she gazed at the boy; then softly she spoke to Elijah. "Now I know you are a man of God, and the message you bring from him is the truth."

Soon Ahab was to make the same discovery.

1 KINGS 18:1–2, 19–46

Elijah and the Prophets of Baal

After three years, God said to Elijah, "Go again to Ahab to give him my message."

Bravely Elijah obeyed. "God will send rain," he told Ahab. "But first you, your people, and your priests must meet me on Mount Carmel."

If Ahab wanted rain, he would have to obey God. Angrily Ahab sent orders out to all the people.

Soon a great crowd was assembled on Mount Carmel.

Elijah spoke. "You cannot have two gods. Either Baal or the Lord God of Israel is the true God. Choose!"

The people gazed at him. No one moved or spoke.

Elijah tried again. "I'm the only one here who serves the Lord. Over there stand four hundred and fifty priests of Baal. Let them choose two young bulls. They will prepare one for sacrifice. I will prepare the other. We will lay the sacrifices on two separate altars. We will light no fire under either of them. Then you pray to Baal, and I will pray to the Lord God. The god who answers with fire shall be the one true God."

The people shouted, "Yes, yes!" The priests of Baal dared not refuse the challenge.

The two bulls were killed and prepared for sacrifice. The priests of Baal stood around their altar. "O Baal, hear us. Send fire," they prayed.

Nothing happened. The priests of Baal began to jump and dance around their altar.

Nothing happened. At midday Elijah began to mock them. "You'd better call louder. He is a god, isn't he? Maybe he's gone on a journey. Or maybe he's asleep. You'll have to wake him up."

133

Furiously the priests of Baal continued their cries. They cut themselves with knives until their blood ran. They knocked down the second altar as they leaped about.

When evening came with still no sign, Elijah gathered the people around him. He went to the altar which had been broken down and built it up using twelve stones, one for each of the tribes of Israel. Then he dug a deep trench all around the altar. He arranged the wood for the fire and placed the sacrifice on the altar. Then he ordered barrels of water to be poured over the sacrifice.

Pour on water? thought the people in surprise. How could a fire burn if everything was soaked with water?

Yet they dared not disobey. The water ran down and filled the trench all around the altar.

When everything was thoroughly soaked, Elijah spoke to God. "Lord God of Abraham, of Isaac, and of Israel, let it be known today that you are the one true God and I am your servant, so that the people may turn from their false gods and worship you."

As he finished speaking, there was a mighty flash of flame. With a great roar, the fire burned up the sacrifice, the altar, and even the water in the trench. Nothing remained.

The people fell on their faces, crying, "The Lord is God! The Lord is God!"

The priests of Baal were put to death. Elijah spoke to the people again. "Go home and eat and drink, because I can hear the sound of rain. The drought and the famine will end."

Ahab went off for a meal, but Elijah climbed to the top of the mountain. There was still no rain. He said to his servant, "Look out to sea. Are there any clouds coming?"

Six times the man looked and saw nothing. But the seventh time the servant called down to Elijah, "There is a cloud. It's about as big as a man's hand."

"Run!" Elijah commanded. "Tell Ahab if he doesn't set off at once his chariot will be overwhelmed by rain."

Now the sky was black with clouds. The wind began to blow. Rain pelted down. Ahab drove off in his chariot, rushing back to his palace.

Excitement filled Elijah, and power from God came to him. So he tucked his garment up into his belt and ran all the way back. He reached the palace ahead of Ahab and his chariot.

But his excitement was soon to change.

Jezebel and Elijah

Still shaken by the happenings on Mount Carmel, King Ahab told the story to his wife Jezebel.

Jezebel had worshiped Baal. When she heard that Baal's priests had been killed, she sent a heated message to Elijah, threatening to kill him.

Elijah fled, taking his servant with him as far as Beersheba. Then he went alone on a day's journey into the desert. Exhausted, he sank down under a juniper tree. "I can't take any more," he groaned. "Let me die."

He fell asleep, miserable and worn out. A gentle touch on his shoulder awoke him. An angel stood beside him. "Eat your meal," said the angel.

Meal? Elijah looked around. There beside him was newly baked bread and a jar of cool water.

Elijah ate and drank. Comforted, he slept once more.

A second time the angel prepared a meal for him. "Eat," said the angel. "You will need strength for your journey."

Elijah obeyed. Then he traveled on for forty days and forty nights until at last he reached Mount Horeb. There he took refuge in a cave.

All night Elijah slept in the cave.

In the morning God spoke to him. "What are you doing here, Elijah?"

The words burst from Elijah. "I've done my very best, working for you. The Israelites have killed all your other prophets. I'm the only one left. And now they're trying to kill me."

"Go out and stand on the mountain before the Lord," said God.

Leave his hiding place? Stand alone before the Lord? Elijah trembled as he went to the front of the cave.

He heard a great and powerful wind tear past the cave. But God was not in the wind.

A rumbling earthquake shook the ground. But God was not in the earthquake.

A fire sprang up. But God was not in the fire.

After the fire and the noise, there was a silence. And in the silence, Elijah heard a still, small voice.

Then Elijah pulled his garment around him and went to the entrance of the cave.

"What are you doing here, Elijah?" the voice asked again.

Quietly Elijah repeated his earlier reply.

God said, "Go back. Your work for me is almost finished. Anoint Hazael as king of Syria. Anoint Jehu as king of Israel. Then anoint Elisha, son of Shaphat, to be my prophet after you."

Greatly heartened, Elijah set out. He found Elisha and dropped his mantle, or cloak, over Elisha's shoulders as a sign that Elisha was to follow him. So Elisha went with Elijah to become his servant.

Then God gave Elijah another task.

Naboth's Vineyard and the Departure of Elijah

King Ahab wanted the vineyard next to his palace, but its owner, Naboth, refused to sell it.

When Queen Jezebel heard what had happened, she schemed with the elders of Jezreel to have Naboth declared guilty of speaking against both King Ahab and God. Naboth was stoned to death.

Ahab took possession of the vineyard, but God sent Elijah to give him terrible news. "Your blood shall be spilled where Naboth died, and Jezebel's body will be eaten by dogs at the wall of Jezreel."

The message came true. God gave Elijah more messages, and Elijah faithfully delivered them until at last he knew his work on earth was done.

"I'll never leave you," declared Elisha, his assistant.

Elijah knew the two of them must be parted. "What can I give you before I go?" he asked gently.

"Give me your spirit," Elisha said, trying to hold in his tears. "Give me a double portion."

This gift was what a father usually gave to his oldest son.

Elijah said, "If you see that which is about to happen, then you will know God has chosen you to be his prophet. You will have what you ask."

Suddenly a chariot and horses of fire appeared. Elijah was lifted into the sky. And Elisha did see it.

"My father!" he cried desperately. Then he picked up Elijah's mantle, or cloak, which had fallen to the ground. He put it on. Elisha knew he was a prophet of God, appointed to continue Elijah's work.

2 KINGS 5:1–15, 19; 13:14–20; 25:10–11

Naaman Is Healed

Naaman was a great man, commander of the king of Syria's army. But he had caught the dreaded disease leprosy, and it seemed there was no hope of a cure.

But Naaman's wife had a young slave girl who had been captured and brought from Israel.

"If only my master would go to the prophet who is in Samaria, he could be healed," the girl said earnestly.

It was worth trying.

Naaman's horses and chariots soon arrived at the door of Elisha's house. Elisha sent out a message. "Go and immerse yourself seven times in the River Jordan, and you will be healed."

"What?" Naaman replied, feeling insulted. "Aren't our own rivers better than the Jordan? I thought the prophet himself would come out and heal me." Then he turned to go home.

But Naaman's servants persuaded him to try doing what Elisha had told him to do.

Naaman was cured.

Humbly he went back to Elisha. "Now I know that your God is the true God, and I will worship him," he vowed.

After a long life of serving God, Elisha died.

Time passed. Many kings ruled in Judah. The people did not worship the true God, and hard times came upon them. Eventually Jerusalem was destroyed, and the people were taken as captives to Babylon where they were very unhappy. But God had not forgotten them. Among the Israelites taken to Babylon was the boy Daniel.

Shadrach, Meshach, and Abednego

Nebuchadnezzar, king of Babylon, chose some of the most clever and handsome children from among his captives, and he ordered that they should live in the palace as members of his household. Four of these were Daniel, Shadrach, Meshach, and Abednego.

The four boys never forgot God. So when Shadrach, Meshach, and Abednego were ordered to worship the golden statue which Nebuchadnezzar had built, they refused. They worshiped God and no one else.

Nebuchadnezzar was furious. He ordered that they be tied up and thrown into a fiery furnace, a furnace so hot that the heat killed the men who threw them in. Yet Shadrach, Meshach, and Abednego stood unbound and unharmed in the middle of the flames.

Nebuchadnezzar was overcome with awe. "I see four men walking in the fire," he whispered, "and the fourth looks like a divine being."

He called for the three to come out of the fire, and not one hair of their heads was the least bit burned.

Nebuchadnezzar ordered that in the future no one was to speak against the God of Israel, and the three men were given important jobs in Babylon.

When Nebuchadnezzar died, his son Belshazzar became king. Belshazzar gave a great feast where something extraordinary happened.

Belshazzar's Feast

King Belshazzar's feast was a merry success. All the guests were enjoying themselves. Suddenly the king turned pale with fear. A hand was writing a message on the wall!

Terrified, the king cried, "Whoever can tell me what this message means shall become third ruler in the land."

His wise men were unable to explain the message. Then the queen remembered Daniel. He had sometimes interpreted dreams and riddles for Nebuchadnezzar.

The king sent for Daniel. Refusing all the rewards, Daniel quietly told him the meaning of the writing on the wall. God had judged Belshazzar's deeds and found them utterly unworthy. Belshazzar's kingdom would fall and be divided among his enemies, the Medes and Persians.

Daniel's words came true. That same night the Medes attacked Babylon. Belshazzar was killed, and Babylon was conquered.

But Daniel's work for God was not over.

Daniel in the Lion's Den

Darius, king of the mighty Medes and Persians, needed someone to be chief ruler in captured Babylon. He knew that Daniel was brave, wise, and honest and would make a good ruler.

The other rulers were furious, and they worked out a trap to catch Daniel.

The Medes and Persians worshiped many gods, but Daniel worshiped only the God of Israel.

The nervous rulers approached the king with the first phase of their plan.

"O King, live forever," they began. "All the rulers have agreed that you should make a law saying that for thirty days no one should pray to any god or man except you. If anyone disobeys the law, he should he thrown to the lions."

King Darius was flattered. The rulers must think him a great king, if they wanted this law. He smiled and nodded.

The rulers hadn't finished. "This law should be written down immediately," they declared.

King Darius nodded again. "Very well," he said.

The rulers watched him write, for once a law of the Medes and Persians was written down, it could never be altered.

The law was made known. As soon as Daniel heard it, he knew it was a trap. He must either give up his daily prayers to God or be thrown to the lions.

With his head held high, he walked boldly down the road toward his home, knowing that his enemies were watching him. He could save his life by not praying to God for thirty days. He could save it by praying secretly in his head. He could try to find a hiding place and pray there.

He walked into his house. He went upstairs to the front room where he always prayed. Boldly he opened the windows, and then

Daniel prayed to God for help.

His enemies in the street below saw him and rushed back to tell the king.

When King Darius heard the news, he saw the trap which had been laid for Daniel. Greatly distressed because Daniel was a favorite of his, he tried to find a way out, but it was no use. He had written the law himself, and it was unchangeable.

That evening the rulers came back and reminded him that the law must be carried out. So the king consented, and Daniel was brought to the edge of the lions' den.

Below, the hungry lions paced back and forth, roaring. Trusting God, Daniel waited.

The men threw him into the den, and the king cried out, "Daniel, may the God to whom you are so faithful save you!"

Hardly able to bear it, Darius watched as a huge stone was rolled into place over the entrance to the den. The king had to seal the stone with his own ring, so that everyone would know if the stone had been moved in a rescue attempt.

Afterward King Darius made his way back to the palace. All night he was tormented by his thoughts. At the very first sign of dawn, he hurried back to the lions' den.

Then he stopped short. What would he see? Had his friend been torn to pieces? Fearfully he made himself call out. "Daniel, has your God saved you?"

He waited. Then Daniel's voice came strong and clear. "O King, live forever. I am safe. God did not let the lions harm me."

Overjoyed, King Darius shouted, "Get Daniel out!"

The men who had thrown Daniel into the den now lifted him out. He was completely untouched by the lions. King Darius ordered that Daniel's accusers and their families be thrown into the lions' den.

Then King Darius wrote for all the people in his kingdom to see, "I command that everyone should respect Daniel's God, for he is great and will last forever."

147

Rebuilding the Temple and Walls of Jerusalem

Many years after the destruction of Jerusalem, Cyrus, king of the Persians, issued a proclamation. God had ordered him to see that the Temple was rebuilt in Jerusalem. Cyrus was also freeing all Jews who had been captured as slaves.

With great rejoicing, thousands of Judeans, or Jews, made the long journey back to their own land.

There they began to repair the city of Jerusalem. After many months, the people started to rebuild the Temple. Throughout the reign of Cyrus, enemies tried to stop the rebuilding. When Darius became king, he ordered that the Jews be allowed to work without harassment.

At last the Temple was finished. It was splendid. But Jerusalem still had no mighty walls to protect the city.

Nehemiah, cupbearer to the king of Persia, got permission from the king to have the walls rebuilt, and he inspired the Jewish people to keep on with the task in spite of all the difficulties put in their way by their enemies.

Finally, with God's help, the work was completed. The walls stood triumphantly.

God continued to care about the people he had created and to be hurt by their disobedience. Now he looked at the wicked city of Nineveh and knew he must find someone to take a message of warning to its people.

Jonah

God spoke to Jonah. "Jonah, I want you to go to the city of Nineveh and tell the people there that they are so wicked that their city is going to be destroyed."

"Me?" cried Jonah. He imagined himself giving such a message. The people would probably kill him. No, no, he couldn't go. Anyway, God was kind and merciful. Surely he'd never destroy a whole city.

"I must get away," thought Jonah. "If I stay here, God will know I'm disobeying him. I'll leave by ship."

So Jonah hurried down to the port of Joppa, and there he found a ship about to sail for Tarshish. Perfect, he thought, I'll go in the opposite direction of Nineveh.

Afraid God might stop him, Jonah paid his fare to the captain and went below. He thought he was safely out of God's sight.

Relieved after all his worrying, Jonah lay down and went to sleep.

149

The ship set sail. Suddenly a great storm blew up. The crew was terrified. They all knelt and prayed to their gods, but still the ship tossed violently on the huge waves.

Making his way below to check the hold, the captain discovered Jonah still sleeping soundly.

"Wake up!" The captain shook him. "We are in deadly peril. Pray to your God, and maybe he will save us."

The sailors had already decided Jonah must be the reason for the storm. As he clambered up onto the deck, they shouted, "Who are you? Where are you from? What is your country?"

"I'm a Hebrew," Jonah answered. "I worship the God who made the sea and the earth. I was trying to run away from God."

The crew was even more terrified.

"Throw me overboard," said Jonah. "Then the sea will be calm."

The sailors looked at one another. Throw a man overboard? Was there no other way? "We'll row for the shore," they said. They went to their stations and heaved on the oars with all their strength, but the storm grew even worse.

Then the sailors cried out to God, "Lord, please don't blame us for killing an innocent man." They picked up Jonah and threw him into the sea.

Immediately the storm died away.

The sailors were very frightened. They offered a sacrifice to God and promised to serve him.

Meanwhile, Jonah was sinking under the water, sure that he would drown. But God sent a huge fish, like a whale, which swallowed Jonah in one gulp. Coughing and gasping, Jonah tried to get his breath back. He was in total darkness. He was inside the enormous fish.

But Jonah was alive. He began to pray to God. Jonah realized how stupid he'd been to think there was any way that he could hide from God. Even though he'd disobeyed God, God had saved his life. Jonah was grateful.

For three miserable, uncomfortable days, Jonah lived inside the fish. Then, at God's command, the fish gave a great belch and spit Jonah onto the shore.

God spoke to him again. "Jonah, go to Nineveh. Give the people my message."

This time Jonah couldn't get there fast enough. When he reached Nineveh, he gave the people God's message. To Jonah's surprise, they believed him at once. The king also believed and commanded that everyone in the city should pray to God for forgiveness. To show they were truly sorry, they took off their fine clothes and wore sackcloth. They did not eat or drink.

God forgave them and did not destroy Nineveh.

Jonah was furious. "I knew that's how it would be!" he declared. "I went through all this for nothing." And he went into the desert, sat down, and sulked.

God made a bushy plant grow up behind him to give him shade. But the next day while Jonah was still sitting there, God commanded a worm to attack the plant.

The plant withered and died. Jonah was sorry for it and angry that it had died so soon. The sun's rays beat down on him, and the scorching wind blew over him. He began to feel so ill that he lay down and prepared to die.

Then God spoke gently to Jonah. "You felt sorry for the plant when it died so soon. Yet you didn't plant it, and you didn't care for it. Think how much more sorry I would have been to destroy the people of Nineveh and their animals, for I made them and love them. Do you really think that I should not have let them live?"

Words from Micah

"He (God) has shown you, O man, what is good; and what does the Lord require of you but to do what is just, to love mercy, and to walk humbly with your God."

The New Testament

The Angel Gabriel Visits Mary

For Mary, the day had begun just like any other. She lived in the small town of Nazareth in Galilee and was engaged to be married to Joseph, the local carpenter. Joseph was honest and kind. She loved him very much.

As Mary sat thinking, the angel Gabriel suddenly appeared to her. "God is with you," he said. "You have found favor with him."

Mary was terrified. But the angel said, "Don't be afraid, Mary. God loves you. You are going to have a baby son, and you must name him Jesus. He will be called the Son of the Most High. God will give him a kingdom. And this kingdom will never end."

Mary tried to calm herself and to understand.

"How can I have a son?" she asked. "I am not yet married."

"The spirit of God will come upon you," Gabriel answered. "The child which shall be born will be the Son of God. Your cousin Elizabeth is also going to have a child, although she has grown old and people say it is impossible. With God nothing is impossible."

Mary listened. All her life she had loved and trusted God. She took a deep breath. "I will do anything that God asks of me," she said.

After the angel left her, Mary sat for some time, trying to take in the tremendous news. Elizabeth—the angel had mentioned Elizabeth.

Mary prepared for a journey. She would go and visit her cousin.

Mary Visits Elizabeth

Elizabeth was married to a man called Zacharias (sometimes written Zechariah), a priest of the Temple. Elizabeth had often prayed for a son. Now as Mary came into the house and greeted her, Elizabeth was full of joy, for she had just felt her baby move inside her.

"How blessed am I!" she said. "The mother of the Son of God has come to see me. And you, Mary, are blessed indeed."

Mary could see it was true that Elizabeth was going to have a child. Her cousin's words helped Mary to accept what was happening. The two women hugged each other.

Elizabeth said, "Let me tell you about my baby. Zacharias was in the Temple one day when the angel Gabriel came and told him I would have a baby son, whom we must call John. Our son is going to be special, Mary. When he grows up, he will tell the people to be ready because their Savior, the Messiah, is coming."

156

Mary listened quietly as Elizabeth continued to speak. "Zacharias wouldn't believe what the angel told him because we're both so old. So the angel made Zacharias speechless. He can't say a word. When he wants something, he has to make signs or write on a tablet."

Mary said softly, "My soul praises the Lord God, and my spirit rejoices in him. He has done great things for me."

Mary stayed on with Elizabeth for about three months before returning to Nazareth. Soon afterward, Elizabeth's baby was born. Her friends and relatives thought she would name him Zacharias, after his father.

"No!" Elizabeth insisted. "He is to be called John."

Her relatives made signs to Zacharias about the name, sure he would agree with them. But Zacharias wrote on his tablet: His name *is* John.

Suddenly Zacharias found that he could speak again. He joyfully began to praise God. Soon everyone in Judea had heard the story and wondered about it.

"Surely God is with this child," they said.

But Mary's baby was yet to be born.

The King Is Born

When Joseph heard that Mary was expecting a child, he was puzzled and distressed. He loved her too much to hurt her, but the proper thing for him to do was to break the engagement.

Then God sent an angel to Joseph in a dream. "Joseph," said the angel, "do not be afraid to take Mary as your wife. The Holy Spirit has come upon her, and she will have a son. You must name him Jesus, which means 'Savior,' because he will save the people from their sins."

Joseph was reassured, and he and Mary began to make preparations for the arrival of the baby. One day, as the time of the birth was drawing near, Joseph came home with bad news.

Caesar Augustus, the Roman ruler, wanted to know exactly how many people were living under Rome's command. Everyone was ordered to go and be counted in the place from which their families came. Wives were to go with their husbands.

Joseph's family was from Bethlehem in Judea. Bethlehem was more than one hundred miles from Nazareth.

No Room

There was no way to avoid the journey. So Joseph and Mary set out for Bethlehem, with Mary riding on a donkey.

Many other people were making the same journey. Because Mary and Joseph had to travel slowly, they arrived long after most of the other travelers. They wondered where they would find lodging.

Joseph led the donkey through the narrow, bustling streets to an inn. He knocked on the door. The innkeeper threw open the door. "No room," he said and started to close the door.

Then he saw Mary. The innkeeper felt very sorry for her. "The inn is full," he said. "But there is room in the stable. The lady would at least be sheltered there, if you don't mind being with the animals."

"Anywhere," said Mary gratefully.

And so it was that God's son was born in a stable in Bethlehem. Mary wrapped him in soft, warm swaddling cloths and laid him tenderly on the sweet-smelling hay in the manger.

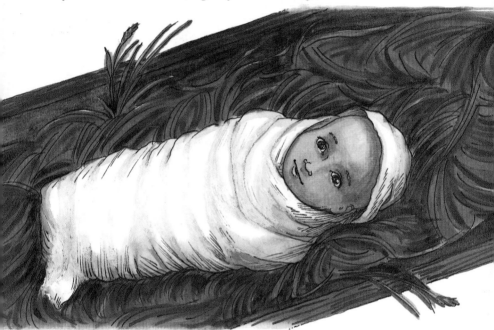

The Visit of the Shepherds

On the hills around Bethlehem, shepherds kept their sheep. On the night Jesus was born, the shepherds were out on the hillside as usual. It was a clear, quiet night.

All at once a bright, glorious light filled the sky. Its brilliance woke the shepherds, and they covered their faces in fear. Then they heard the beautiful voice of an angel of the Lord.

"Do not be afraid. I have good news for you and all people. For unto you is born this day in the city of David a Savior who is Christ the Lord. And this will be a sign to you. You will find the baby wrapped in swaddling cloths, lying in a manger."

Then the whole sky filled with angels saying, "Glory to God in

159

the highest, and on earth peace and goodwill toward men."

The light and the angels' voices faded, and there was silence.

The shepherds tried to take in what they'd seen and heard. The city of David meant Bethlehem. Was it true that the Savior had been born in Bethlehem?

The shepherds left their sheep and raced toward Bethlehem.

They came to the inn and saw a dim light shining from the stable. Trembling, they looked inside.

In the manger, wrapped in warm cloths exactly as the angel had said, lay baby Jesus. Quietly the shepherds knelt to worship.

They told Mary and Joseph about the message of the angels. As dawn broke, the shepherds returned to their flocks, joyously telling the good news to everyone they met.

When the time came, Joseph and Mary prepared to take baby Jesus to be presented in the Temple in Jerusalem as God commanded in the laws written down by Moses.

Simeon and Anna in the Temple

In Jerusalem there lived an old man named Simeon. God had promised him he would not die until he had seen the Messiah, the Savior for whom the Jewish people were waiting. At last God said, "Go to the Temple, Simeon. Today you will find the Messiah there."

Trembling with excitement, Simeon made his way to the Temple as fast as he could. When he saw the baby Jesus, he knew he had found the Messiah.

"Please, may I hold him?" he asked Mary. As he took the baby in his arms, Simeon praised God. Then he blessed Joseph and Mary.

Gently he handed the baby back to Mary. A very old lady named Anna, who never left the Temple, came up to them at that moment.

"This is the Messiah!" she proclaimed. She thanked God and told the people around her that the Savior had come.

Mary and Joseph carried out the ceremony of presenting the baby to God, which the Law demanded.

But there were still other surprises to come. This young child was to receive very special visitors.

The Wise Men and the Flight into Egypt

King Herod sat in his palace in Jerusalem, knowing nothing of the angels, the shepherds, or the extraordinary things which had been happening to Mary and Joseph. Then one day, wise men from far away to the east asked for an audience with Herod.

Politely the wise men bowed low. "Where is the new baby king?" they asked. "As we studied the sky, we saw his star rise in the east, and we have come to worship him."

A new baby king to replace him? Herod went pale with rage and fear. He ordered his chief priests and lawyers to search in their books. "Find out where this new king is to be born!" he commanded.

They soon returned with the answer: "In Bethlehem of Judea."

Herod took the wise men to one side. "Go to Bethlehem," he said. "Search carefully for the child. When you've found him, come back and tell me where he is. I want to worship him too."

Unaware of Herod's true feelings, the wise men left the palace. When they arrived in Bethlehem, they found Mary, Joseph, and Jesus.

Mary and Joseph watched in astonishment as these splendid travelers from foreign lands knelt and worshiped the child. They watched as the wise men presented him with rich gifts of gold, frankincense, and myrrh. Gold was a present given to kings. Frankincense was burned on the altar of the Lord. And myrrh was used to help preserve the bodies of the people when they died. Mary shuddered. Why were these wise men giving her baby myrrh?

It was late now. As the wise men rested for the night, God sent them a dream.

"Do not go back to King Herod. He means to harm the child."

So in the morning the wise men departed and obeyed God's instruction to keep away from Herod.

Joseph also had a dream. An angel appeared to him and said, "Get up. Take the boy and his mother and escape into Egypt. Stay there until I tell you it is safe to return, for Herod means to kill the child."

Joseph woke with a start. "Mary!" he whispered urgently. "Wake up! We must take the child and leave at once." And he told Mary about his dream.

Soon the donkey was saddled, their few possessions were bundled up, and the sleepy boy was wrapped warmly.

They set out in the starlight, hurrying along the streets of Bethlehem with only the clip-clop of the donkey's hooves breaking the silence. Would they escape?

The Boy Jesus

God's warning had come in time. Joseph, Mary, and Jesus reached Egypt in safety.

But when Herod discovered he had been outwitted by the wise men, he was furious. He ordered that every boy two years old or younger who lived in or near Bethlehem be killed.

There was great weeping and mourning in Bethlehem, but Herod was soon satisfied that no baby king existed to threaten his throne.

Meanwhile, in Egypt, Jesus grew bigger and stronger.

At last King Herod died, and an angel again appeared to Joseph in a dream. It was now safe to leave Egypt.

So Mary, Joseph, and Jesus went to Nazareth in Galilee. There Joseph again took up his work as a carpenter.

When Jesus was old enough, he went to school in Nazareth. On the Sabbath, he went to the synagogue with Joseph. Mary went as well, but she sat with the other women, as was the custom.

As Jesus grew older, he listened very carefully to all he heard in the synagogue. And he asked a lot of questions.

Every year Joseph and Mary went to the Temple in Jerusalem for the Feast of the Passover, the time when Jews remembered their escape from Egypt during the days of Moses. When Jesus was twelve years old, he went with them to Jerusalem.

When the festival was over, Joseph and Mary set out for home. They were with a large group of people from Nazareth. As usual, the women and children walked in one part of the group and the men and older boys in another. Neither Joseph nor Mary worried because Jesus was not in sight. Each thought he was with the other one.

All day they traveled. It was not until the people began to set up camp for the night that Joseph and Mary realized Jesus was missing.

No one had seen Jesus since the group had left Jerusalem.

Deeply distressed, Mary and Joseph hurried back to the city. It was still full of people.

For three days they scoured Jerusalem. At last they entered the Temple, almost without hope. What twelve-year-old boy would want to spend time there?

Mary and Joseph stopped in amazement. There was Jesus, sitting among the wise men of Jerusalem. He was talking to them and asking them questions. The men were astonished at the kind of questions he asked and the amount he understood.

After a moment Mary moved forward. "Son, why have you behaved like this? We've been searching everywhere for you!"

Jesus was surprised. "Why were you searching? I thought you would know I was here in my Father's house."

Joseph and Mary looked at him, unable to understand. "Come home with us now," they said.

They went back to Nazareth and life went on as usual.

But Jesus knew he must soon leave home and start on the task for which he had come.

His cousin John had already begun.

The Baptism of Jesus

John, son of Elizabeth and Zacharias, grew up seeing much of life in the Temple in Jerusalem where his father was a priest.

But John felt that the Temple, with all its rules and regulations, wasn't the place for him. So as soon as he was old enough, he left.

He went into the desert to live by himself, and there God spoke to him. John believed God's words. The Messiah, the Savior, was coming soon, and it was John's task to tell everyone. John was to prepare the people to listen to the Messiah when he did come.

While still in the desert, John started to preach to the people.

"Prepare, for the Kingdom of Heaven is to come soon. Confess to the wrong things you have done. Show that you are sorry by living a better life. Come and be baptized."

To be "baptized" meant to be "washed," or dipped in the water as a sign that the wrong things in a person's life were being washed away. Because he baptized, John was given the name "John the Baptist."

People in the towns began talking about John.

"He wears clothes made from camel hair. He lives in the desert and eats locusts and wild honey. He's preaching a new message."

Soon crowds of people were going to see John. Many of them believed John's message, and John baptized them in the River Jordan.

Some people wondered if John was the Savior, the Messiah for whom the Jews had long been waiting. John told them he was not.

"I baptize you with water," he said, "but someone is coming who is much more powerful than I am. I'm not fit even to untie his sandals. He will baptize you with fire and with the Holy Spirit."

Jesus heard about his cousin John's preaching and came from Galilee to the River Jordan to be baptized.

When John saw Jesus, he felt God speaking to him. And John cried out, "Look! Here is the one I've been telling you about. He is

166

the one who will take away the sins of the world!"

Quietly Jesus came up to John. But John said, "No, you should baptize me. You are much greater than I am."

Jesus answered softly, "This is the way God wishes it to be."

So John baptized Jesus in the River Jordan.

Jesus's baptism was different from everyone else's because he had done no wrong which needed to be washed away. As he came back onto the bank, the sky was opened and the Spirit of God came down to him in the shape of a dove.

God's voice was heard. "This is my beloved son, in whom I am well-pleased."

Then Jesus was full of the Holy Spirit. And he knew he must go into the wilderness for a while to be by himself and to prepare for the work which he had come to earth to do.

Jesus in the Wilderness

For forty days and forty nights, Jesus stayed in the wilderness. He thought deeply about the power which God had given him and how he should use it. He ate nothing in all that time.

At the end of forty days, Satan tempted him. "Look at these stones. If you are really the Son of God, turn these stones into bread."

Jesus was very hungry. But he knew his power had not been given to him to use for himself.

"Man shall not live by bread alone, but also by the word of God," he answered from Scripture.

Satan tried again. He took Jesus to the highest ledge of the Temple in Jerusalem. "If you are really the Son of God," whispered Satan, "throw yourself off this ledge." Satan then spoke from Scripture. "It is written, 'God will order his angels to take care of you. They will not let you even bruise your foot on a stone.'"

Jesus answered, "But it is also written, 'Do not tempt God.'"

Satan then led Jesus to a very high place.

"Look," he whispered. "You can see all the kingdoms of the world from here. I will give you authority over all the world and all the splendor of the world if you worship me."

But Jesus answered, "Go away, Satan! It is written, 'You shall worship the Lord your God, and him only shall you serve.'"

Satan gave up for the moment, waiting for another opportunity.

Angels came to Jesus and took care of him.

Then Jesus went back to Galilee. All through the countryside, people began to tell one another about the things he said and did.

They wanted to see and hear more.

MATTHEW 9:9–13; 10:1–4; LUKE 5:1–11, 27–32; HOSEA 6:6

Jesus's Disciples

Except in his own village of Nazareth, the people of Galilee crowded around Jesus to listen to him wherever he went.

One day four fishermen, Simon, Andrew, James, and John, were at the shore of the Sea of Galilee. They were gloomily cleaning their nets. They went out fishing at night because that was usually the best time to catch fish. But last night they'd caught nothing.

Now as they worked on the nets, they heard a commotion. Looking up, they saw Jesus coming with a crowd of people following him.

Jesus came up to Simon and asked, "May I borrow your boat?"

Gladly Simon agreed.

Jesus then asked Simon to row a short distance out from shore. Then Jesus sat down and began to speak to the people.

The crowd settled down to listen. The four fishermen listened too.

When Jesus had finished teaching the people, he turned to Simon and said, "Sail out to the deep water, and there let down your nets."

Simon hesitated. "Master, we've fished all night, and we haven't caught a thing. But I'll do as you say."

Andrew, Simon's brother, waded out and climbed into the boat as well. They sailed out and let down the nets.

Suddenly there was a great tugging on the nets. Simon and Andrew began to haul in their catch. The nets were so full of fish that they began to break.

James and John quickly rowed their boat over to help. They were all trying desperately to get the fish on board. There were so many fish that both boats came close to sinking under the weight of them.

Jesus said to Simon, "From now on you will catch men, not fish."

Simon understood that Jesus meant for him to help in the work of telling men about God's message.

As quickly as they could, Simon, Andrew, James, and John landed their boats safely on the shore. Then they left everything and followed Jesus to become his special helpers, his disciples.

Jesus needed more disciples. He saw Matthew, a tax collector, sitting at his table collecting taxes.

To Matthew's amazement, Jesus stopped to speak to him. Jesus was a Jew, and most Jews hated the tax collectors. Not only did the tax collectors cheat by taking more money than was due, they worked for the Romans, who had occupied the country and now ruled it.

But Jesus said, "Follow me."

Jesus wanted him? Matthew could hardly believe it. He gladly jumped up, leaving everything behind as the others had done.

A little while later, Matthew gave a party which Jesus attended.

Some of the Pharisees, Jews who were very strict in the way they kept the laws of Moses, saw the party. They were shocked. They said to the disciples, "How can your leader possibly eat with people like that—tax collectors and people who don't keep the law?"

Jesus overheard them. "People who are well don't need a doctor," he said. "I came to give God's message to everyone, not just to respectable people."

Jesus chose other disciples, until finally he had an inner group of twelve: Simon Peter, Andrew, James, John, Philip, Nathaniel (or Bartholomew), Matthew, Thomas, James (son of Alphaeus), Thaddaeus, Simon the Zealot, and Judas Iscariot.

JOHN 2:1–11
The Wedding at Cana

There was a wedding at Cana in Galilee. Jesus's mother, Mary, was one of the guests, and Jesus and his disciples had also been invited. The party was going splendidly. Then Mary came over to Jesus and whispered anxiously, "Jesus, the wine is all gone! There's none left!"

The host and hostess would be very ashamed because they had run out of wine. They would remember it with shame every time they remembered the wedding.

Mary was certain that Jesus would help his friends. The servants were standing nearby. So Mary said to them, "Do as Jesus tells you."

There were six huge stone jars standing in the corner of the room.

"Fill those jars with fresh water," Jesus said to the servants. "Then pour some out and offer it to the chief guest."

172

Offer water to the chief guest? The servants hesitated, but then did as Jesus said. They watched anxiously as the guest took a sip.

"Well!" exclaimed the chief guest. "Most people serve their best wine first and keep the worst until last. But you have kept the best wine until last."

The water had been turned into wine, and there was plenty of it.

Everyone smiled and laughed, and the party continued.

Jesus had performed his first miracle in Cana of Galilee. His disciples saw it, and they began to trust him completely.

Soon Jesus would perform other miracles.

The Man Who Couldn't Walk

There was a man living in Capernaum who was paralyzed so that he couldn't walk. His friends knew he was unhappy because he couldn't get around and had to beg for a living. But he was also unhappy because he knew he had done many wrong things in his life.

One day four of his friends came rushing up. "Jesus is in Capernaum," they said. "He's healing sick people."

Then each of his four friends grabbed a corner of his bed, and they carried him off to find Jesus.

When they reached Capernaum, it was easy to tell which house Jesus was in. There was a huge crowd of people around the doorway, all trying to hear what Jesus was saying to the Pharisees and teachers inside the house.

"Please, let us through," said the four friends.

But no one would give way.

Then the four friends had an idea. They carried the man, still on his bed, up the outside stairs and onto the flat roof of the house.

They began lifting off some of the roof tiles. Soon they had created an opening large enough for the bed to go through.

Slowly, carefully, the four men lowered their friend through the hole in the roof, using ropes attached to each corner of the bed.

In the room below, Jesus stopped talking. He looked up at this extraordinary sight. The Pharisees and teachers looked up too. They were horrified. How dare anyone behave like this?

The four friends continued to lower the man into the middle of the crowd and right in front of Jesus.

Jesus looked down at the man. And the man looked up at Jesus. Jesus could see the misery and fear in his eyes, and he understood.

"My friend," Jesus said gently, "your sins are all forgiven."

The Pharisees and teachers began thinking, What? He's forgiving sins? He speaks blasphemy! Only God can forgive sins!

Jesus knew what they were thinking. "Which is easier," he asked, "to say 'your sins are forgiven' or to say 'get up and walk'?"

They were silent.

Jesus went on. "So that you can know that I have the power to forgive sins," he said, turning toward the paralyzed man again, "I say to you get up, pick up your bed, and walk."

The man could feel strength flowing into him. He moved his legs. He struggled to his feet and wobbled a little. "Praise God!" he yelled. His face glowing with joy, the man bent to pick up his bed. The next moment he was pushing his way through the crowd.

The four friends came rushing down the stairs and joyfully greeted their friend. Still praising God, he headed home.

"We've seen something amazing happen here today," the people said to one another.

Other amazing things were to happen.

LUKE 7:1–10

The Roman Centurion's Servant

Most Jews hated the Roman soldiers who had overcome their country and now occupied it. But in Capernaum there was one Roman soldier whom they liked and respected.

He was a centurion, in charge of a hundred men. He was a good leader, and he was kind to the Jews. When the Jews' synagogue became too old to use, he had a beautiful new one built for them.

The centurion had a servant whom he valued very much. One day, the servant became very ill and was close to death.

The centurion had heard about Jesus, and he knew that he had healed many people, even those who were dying. But Jesus was a Jew. He might not want to help a Roman.

In desperation, the centurion went to his Jewish friends. He asked them to speak to Jesus for him. Wanting to help the centurion, they went to Jesus.

"Of course I'll come," said Jesus, and they set out together.

While the centurion waited for Jesus to come, he began to feel dreadful. How could he possibly have asked Jesus to take all the trouble of coming to his house? He sent his friends to Jesus with a message.

"Lord," they said, "the centurion says please don't go to the trouble of coming to his house. He feels he doesn't deserve a visit from you, and he's not a good enough person to speak to you. If you'll just say the word, he knows his servant will be healed."

Jesus was amazed. He turned to the crowd of people who were constantly following him. "Listen," he said to them, "I haven't found anyone else with such great faith as this, not even among the Jews."

When the centurion's friends went back to the house, they found that his servant was quite well again.

The Storm on the Sea of Galilee

Jesus had spent most of the day talking to the crowds of people who had gathered to listen to him.

By the time evening came, Jesus was weary, but the crowds still did not leave. It was no use trying to walk away, for they would simply follow him. Jesus had been talking to them near the shores of the Sea of Galilee. Now he noticed the fishing boats on the shore.

"Let's sail over to the other side," Jesus said to his disciples.

So they all climbed into a boat and set sail.

Jesus went to one end of the boat, lay down, and fell asleep.

A sudden storm blew up. The boat began to toss violently. The boat almost capsized as huge waves rose up and crashed down into it. The disciples were terrified, yet Jesus still slept.

The waves lifted the boat high, then tossed it down again. The frightened disciples could bear it no longer. They scrambled down to the end of the boat where Jesus was sleeping.

"Master, wake up!" they cried. "We're in dreadful danger. We're likely to drown. Don't you care?"

Jesus woke up. He stood up straight and unafraid. He said to the storm, "Peace, be still."

Immediately the wind died down. The waves calmed and the water became smooth again.

Jesus turned to look at his disciples. "Why were you afraid? Why didn't you have even a little faith?"

The disciples gazed at him in awe. They whispered to each other, "Who is this man? Even the wind and the waves do as he tells them!"

The boat sailed on. Everyone landed safely on the far shore, where, as usual, people were waiting to ask Jesus to help them.

Jairus's Daughter and the Sick Woman

It was the morning after the storm, and Jesus and his disciples were sailing back across the Sea of Galilee.

When they reached the shore, a crowd was already there, waiting to welcome Jesus. A man named Jairus pushed his way through the crowd and threw himself at Jesus's feet.

"Please," Jairus cried desperately, "come to my house. My daughter is dying. She's only twelve years old. Please come!"

"Of course I'll come," Jesus said. They set out at once. Jairus wanted to run, but the crowds hemmed them in.

Then Jesus suddenly stopped. "Who touched me?" he asked.

His disciple Peter said, "Master, people are all around you."

"Someone touched me in a special way," Jesus insisted. "I felt power going out of me."

A trembling woman knelt at his feet. "I touched you," she confessed. "I've been ill for twelve years, and no one could help me. I knew if I just touched the hem of your robe, I would be healed."

Jesus looked at her with great kindness. "Because you had faith in me, you have been made well," he said.

Jairus watched anxiously. Why didn't Jesus hurry?

But just as Jesus moved toward him, Jairus saw some men coming from his house. A chill went through Jairus.

"Your daughter is dead," they told him.

Jairus was filled with grief. But Jesus said, "Don't be afraid. Trust me, your daughter will be healed."

Then Jesus began to walk quickly toward Jairus's house. Jairus followed, afraid to hope, yet still trusting Jesus.

When they reached the house, a crowd of people had already gathered. Everyone was crying because the child was dead.

"Hush," said Jesus. "She isn't dead. She's only asleep."

"What?" they exclaimed, and they began to laugh at him. Asleep, indeed—as if they couldn't tell whether or not a person was dead!

Jesus sent everyone out of the room except three of his disciples—Peter, James, and John—and the girl's mother and father.

Quietly Jesus took the girl's hand. "Child, wake up," he said.

The girl stirred a little and opened her eyes. Then she sat up. The next moment she was standing up, perfectly well again.

Jesus smiled and said, "Give her something to eat."

His words were so practical that they brought everyone back to their senses. Jairus hugged his daughter while her mother rushed to get a meal ready.

"Don't tell anyone what happened here today," Jesus said.

Then he and his disciples left.

MATTHEW 14:13–23; MARK 6:30–46; LUKE 9:1–3, 6, 10–17;
JOHN 6:1–15

Feeding the Five Thousand

A great crowd of people had gathered to hear Jesus speak. He told the
people about God and his kingdom. He healed the sick people and
told stories to the children who were there.

The day passed. Even though it grew late in the afternoon, the
crowd remained as huge as ever. The disciples began to worry. They
imagined all those people stumbling home in the dark. And the crowd
must be very hungry, for they hadn't eaten all day.

The disciples went to Jesus and said, "Master, we believe you
should tell all these people to leave now so that they can get some
food and find somewhere to spend the night."

"You give them food to eat," Jesus said.

"What?" said Philip, one of the twelve. "It would take eight
months' wages to be able to buy enough bread to feed them all!"

"Find out how much food we have," said Jesus.

The disciples inquired among the people, but they found only five
small barley loaves and two small fish.

Jesus said, "Tell everyone to sit down in groups of hundreds and
fifties."

The disciples looked at one another; then they obeyed. Soon the
people were sitting on the grassy hillside. There were about five
thousand men, and many more women and children.

Jesus took the five loaves and the two fish and gave thanks to
God for them. Then he gave them to the disciples to pass out to the
people.

And there was plenty of food.

When the people couldn't eat any more, Jesus instructed the
disciples to gather up the leftovers. The disciples were amazed as
they collected enough scraps of food to fill twelve baskets.

Jesus saw how tired the disciples were. "Return to the boat and go on ahead of me," he said. "I'll tell the people it's time for them to leave."

But the people were not ready to be sent away. They were talking excitedly among themselves.

"Surely Jesus is the prophet we have been waiting for. Let's make him our king!"

Jesus knew what they were saying, but it was not God's will for him to be king. He quietly left the people and made his way alone further up into the hills. There he prayed.

Meanwhile, his disciples had gone down to the seashore.

Jesus Walks on the Water

It was almost dark. The fishing boat lay waiting at the edge of the water. Some people stood nearby, and they saw the disciples come to the boat. They were surprised to see the disciples without Jesus.

The disciples got into the boat and started to row. It had become quite dark. A strong wind was blowing against them, and the sea was rough. Wearily the disciples pulled on the oars. The journey seemed endless. They rowed for some time, but because of the rough waves they traveled only three or four miles.

By the dim light of the moon, the disciples suddenly saw a figure coming toward them, walking on the water. They did not realize it was Jesus. The disciples froze in terror. "It's a ghost!" they cried out.

At once Jesus spoke to them. "It's me. Don't be afraid."

The disciples strained to see. Peter said, "Master, if it's really you, tell me to walk on the water toward you."

"Come," said Jesus. The disciples watched in silent awe as Peter climbed over the side of the boat and walked toward Jesus. He took a few steps in perfect safety. Then he realized what he was doing, and he was afraid. Immediately he began to sink.

"Lord, save me!" Peter cried.

Instantly Jesus reached out and caught him. "You have so little faith," he said. "Why did you doubt?"

Together they got into the boat. At that same moment, the wind ceased to blow and the sea became calm.

In the moonlight, the disciples looked at Jesus. Reverently they said, "Truly you are the Son of God."

They crossed the Sea of Galilee and came safely to the other side. The next day the people who had seen the disciples leave without Jesus were confused. They said, "Jesus is over on the other shore. But he wasn't in the boat when it left here, and there was only one boat."

Healing the Sick

The Ten Lepers

Jesus was now making his way to Jerusalem through Samaria and Galilee. Ten men who suffered from the disease of leprosy learned that he was going to pass quite close to where they were living.

Leprosy was a dreaded disease because no one knew how to cure it. The disease would eat away at whichever part of the body was affected. Fingers and toes could be lost, and faces disfigured. Everyone was afraid of catching the disease, so lepers were forced to leave their homes and go outside the village to live.

There was no hope for lepers.

But these ten men had heard that Jesus healed sick people. Could he heal them? One of the men, a Samaritan, was also concerned because Jesus was a Jew, and for many years the Jews and the Samaritans had disliked and mistrusted each other.

But the ten lepers resolved to try to reach Jesus.

They watched and waited near the road. At last they saw Jesus coming, and they called out, "Jesus, Master, help us!"

Jesus turned and saw their troubled, desperate faces. He called back to them, "Go and let the priests examine you."

The lepers looked at each other. Go and show themselves to a priest? They'd had to show themselves to a priest when they first caught the disease. It was the priests who decided which people had leprosy. People only went back to the priest if they wanted to prove they were well and didn't have leprosy after all.

But the lepers trusted Jesus, so they set out to find the priests. As they walked along together, their skin cleared and was healed.

Then one of them, the Samaritan, came rushing joyfully back to Jesus. He threw himself down at Jesus's feet. "Thank you! Oh, thank you!" he cried.

Jesus looked down at the Samaritan. "Weren't all ten people

healed?" he asked. "Where are the other nine? Is this foreigner the only one ready to praise God?"

Then gently Jesus spoke to the Samaritan. "Get up and go on your way. Your faith has made you well."

The news about Jesus continued to spread among the people.

Bartimaeus

In Jericho there lived a man named Bartimaeus, who was blind.

He could not find any work. To keep from starving, he sat by the roadside all day, begging for money.

Bartimaeus heard that Jesus was on his way to Jerusalem. He had heard about Jesus and how he healed the sick. But he wondered how he would be able to push his way through the crowds to find a person he couldn't even see.

Disappointment flooded through him. But maybe, if he just sat there and called out to Jesus, he might be able to make himself heard.

For several long, hot, dusty days, Bartimaeus sat by the roadside. Then at last he heard the sounds of an excited crowd.

"What's happening?" he called to the passersby.

"Jesus of Nazareth is coming!" someone answered.

Bartimaeus's heart raced. He waited until he guessed Jesus was passing him, then he shouted, "Jesus, help me!"

Amid all the noise and bustle, Jesus heard Bartimaeus and turned to look for him. Jesus saw that Bartimaeus was blind and unable to make his way through the crowd.

"Bring that man to me!" Jesus said.

Now hands were urging Bartimaeus to get up. He scrambled to his feet and let himself be led into the middle of the crowd, to Jesus.

He heard Jesus ask, "What do you want me to do for you?"

"Oh," Bartimaeus replied, "if only I could see."

Jesus answered, "Then see. Your faith has healed you."

At once light dazzled Bartimaeus. He put up a hand to shade his eyes. He could see the sunshine. He could see the trees, the sky, and the faces of the crowd. He could see Jesus.

Bartimaeus was overjoyed and gave thanks to God. The people all praised God and were glad.

MATTHEW 19:13–15; 20:17–19; MARK 10:13–16, 32–34;
LUKE 18:15–17, 31–34; ISAIAH 53:7–12

Jesus and the Children

The people wanted to ask Jesus to bless their sons and daughters. And the older children longed to see Jesus for themselves. But it wasn't easy to get small children safely through the crowds which usually surrounded Jesus.

One day a group of parents and children came eagerly toward Jesus as he sat and rested for a while. This could be their chance. Excitedly the children tried to run on ahead.

But the disciples turned and saw the little group. "Why are you bothering Jesus with all these children?" the disciples asked harshly.

But Jesus spoke sternly. "What are you doing? Let the children come to me. The Kingdom of Heaven belongs to such as these."

He opened his arms wide, and the children ran to him. He said to the people who were watching, "I tell you all, if you don't receive the Kingdom in the same spirit as a child does, you'll never enter it."

Jesus took the children into his arms and blessed each one. The people who crowded around tried to understand what he was saying. They were to accept God's kingdom in a spirit of trust, the way a young child trusts his or her parents.

The mothers, fathers, and children happily went back to their homes. Jesus and his disciples continued on their way toward Jerusalem. He intended to be there for the Feast of the Passover. But the people were afraid.

When Jesus noticed the disciples' anxious faces, he called them to one side. He knew exactly what was troubling them. The chief priests and the Pharisees had often been angry over the things Jesus said and did. They had decided that Jesus was just an ordinary man, not the Son of God, the Messiah. The priests and Pharisees were afraid that the people would try to make Jesus the king, that there would be trouble with the Romans, and that the priests and Pharisees themselves would suffer. So they were waiting for a chance to kill Jesus. And the disciples thought that if Jesus went to Jerusalem, he would be walking into a trap.

"Listen," Jesus tried to explain. "We are going to Jerusalem. The Son of Man will be handed over to the chief priests and the teachers of the law. He will be condemned to death. They will hand him over to the Roman soldiers, who will mock him, torture him, and crucify him. This must happen, just as the prophets foretold. But three days after his death, the Son of Man will rise to life again."

The disciples listened, but they didn't understand. They only knew that Jesus was quite set in his purpose. They loved him, and if he went to Jerusalem, so would they.

First they had to pass through Jericho and, as usual, someone was waiting eagerly for Jesus to come by.

Luke 19:1–10
Zacchaeus

Zacchaeus was a chief tax collector in Jericho. He was rich, but his money had come from collecting taxes. Sometimes Zacchaeus and the other collectors took more money from the people than was rightfully owed in taxes. Almost all Jews hated tax collectors for this very reason. Zacchaeus had few friends, and he was very lonely.

One day Zacchaeus heard that Jesus was coming.

He longed to see what Jesus looked like. But Zacchaeus was a very short man, and he was standing at the very back of the crowd now lining the road to see Jesus.

Then Zacchaeus had an idea. He ran down the road to a sycamore tree and quickly climbed it. Now he had a perfect view of the road.

Zacchaeus watched the crowd getting closer and closer. Now they were passing by the sycamore tree. Jesus was almost there.

Suddenly Jesus stopped and looked straight up at Zacchaeus. Jesus said, "Zacchaeus, come down. Today I must stay at your house."

Filled with excitement, Zacchaeus came scrambling down.

"You are very welcome in my house," Zacchaeus replied.

Now Zacchaeus was not squeezed to the back of the crowd. He was leading the way with Jesus beside him. When the people saw what Jesus did, they began to mutter, "Look at that! Jesus is actually going to visit the house of a sinner!"

When Zacchaeus heard these words, he stopped. "Master," he said, "I'll give half of my belongings to the poor. And if I've cheated anyone, I'll give him back four times as much."

There was a gasp of surprise from the people. Jesus said to them, "Salvation has come to this house today, for this man is also a son of Abraham. Remember, the Son of Man has come to seek out and save those who have strayed from God."

Zacchaeus heard Jesus's words, and he felt happier than he had ever been before. Gladly Zacchaeus led the way into his house.

After Jesus had visited Zacchaeus, he continued on his way toward Jerusalem.

The Sermon on the Mount

One day when Jesus saw the crowds following him, he went up on a mountainside and sat down. The people gathered all around Jesus, and he taught them. Here are some of the things he said that day.

"Happy and blessed are those who know they must trust in God, for the Kingdom of Heaven shall be theirs.

"Blessed are those who mourn and are sad, for they shall be comforted.

"Blessed are those who are not proud but humble, for they shall inherit the whole earth.

"Blessed are those who greatly desire to do right, for they shall be satisfied.

"Blessed are those who are merciful, for mercy shall be shown to them.

"Blessed are those whose thoughts are pure, for they shall see God.

"Blessed are those who make peace, for they shall be called the children of God.

"Blessed are those who suffer for what they know to be right, for theirs is the Kingdom of Heaven.

"If men persecute you, call you names, and tell lies about you because you love me, rejoice and be glad, for your reward in heaven will be great.

"If you are my followers, you are like salt which gives flavor to food. Or you are like a light for the whole world. So don't hide your light where it can't be seen. When you do good, people will see it, and they will give praise to God your Father.

"You have been told, 'You shall not kill.' But I say to you, thoughts which make you feel like murdering someone are also wrong.

"You have been told, 'An eye for an eye, and a tooth for a tooth.' But I say to you, do not take revenge on anyone who acts wrongly against you.

"You have been told, 'Love your friends, but hate your enemies.' But I say to you, love your enemies. Pray for those who do you wrong. This way you will become sons and daughters of your heavenly Father. For he makes his sun to shine and rain to fall on the good and bad alike. Why should God give you a reward for loving the people who love you? Even tax collectors do that. And if you talk only to your friends, you've done nothing special.

"If you help those who are in need, don't tell everyone about it. Your Father in heaven will see, and he will reward you.

"When you pray, talk quietly to God. He is your Father and knows what you need even before you ask him for it.

"Pray like this: Our Father, who is in heaven, hallowed be your name. Your kingdom come, your will be done, on earth as it is in heaven. Give us this day our daily bread. And forgive us our debts as we forgive our debtors. And lead us not into temptation, but deliver us from evil. For yours is the kingdom, the power, and the glory, forever. Amen.

"And don't worry. Your heavenly Father knows what you need. Put his kingdom first, try to do as he wants, and everything you need will be given to you. Don't worry about tomorrow. Tomorrow will have enough worries of its own.

"Don't judge other people, saying they are right or wrong. If you judge them, you will be judged yourselves. It's as if you saw a speck of sawdust in someone else's eye and never noticed a huge plank of wood in your own eye.

"If your son asked for bread, would you give him a stone? Or if he asked you for a fish, would you give him a snake? If you know how to give good gifts to your children, just think how much more your heavenly Father will give to those who ask him.

"Always treat other people the way you would like them to treat you. This is what the law is about."

As they listened, the people were amazed because Jesus taught them with authority, but not in the usual way of the teachers of the law.

The Parables

Wherever Jesus went, crowds of people gathered to hear him. He often told parables, or stories with special meanings for the people to think about. These are some of the parables Jesus told.

MATTHEW 7:24–27; LUKE 6:47–49

The House on the Rock

"There were two men. Each one wanted to build a house. The first man understood how important it was for his house to have a good, firm foundation. So he dug deep into the ground until he came to solid rock. He laid the foundation on the rock and built his house.

"The second man cared nothing about having a strong foundation for his house. He built it on the sand.

"Soon afterward a storm began to blow. The wind howled and the rain poured down. Rivers overflowed their banks, flooding the land and beating against the walls of the two houses.

196

"The house which was built on the rock had a strong foundation, and it did not fall. But the house which was built on the sand fell down with a mighty crash.

"Anyone who hears my words and lives by them is like the wise man who built his house on the rock. When troubles come, that person will not give in, but will stand firm.

"But anyone who hears my words and does not live by them is like the foolish man who built his house upon the sand. When troubles come, that person will be crushed by them because he does not have anything strong on which to stand."

Luke 8:4–15

The Sower

"A farmer went out to sow some seed. As he walked up and down his field, he scattered handfuls of grain.

"Some seed fell on the path, and the birds ate it.

"Some seed fell on rock where there was little soil. The seeds sprouted, but the young plants could not put down roots. They soon withered and died in the hot sun.

"Some seed fell among thornbushes. The seed grew, but the thorns grew faster, choking out the tender plants.

"But some seed fell on the good, rich earth. The plants put down deep, strong roots. The crop grew tall and ripened in the sun. By harvest time, the plants had produced a hundred times more grain than the farmer had sown."

Jesus's disciples didn't understand the meaning of this parable, so they asked him to explain it.

Jesus replied, "The seed stands for God's Word. Some people listen to God's Word carelessly. Satan can easily make them forget what they've heard. That is the seed which fell on the path.

"Some people listen gladly and believe for a short time. But as soon as trouble comes, they stop believing. That is the seed which fell on the rock and had no roots.

"Some people hear the message, but their minds are so full of other thoughts, worries, and desires that there is no room for God's Word to grow. That is the seed which fell among thorns.

"But some people listen to God's Word and believe it. They make his message part of their hearts, and their lives show that they love and obey God. That is the seed which fell on rich soil."

LUKE 10:25–37

The Good Samaritan

A teacher of the law tried to test Jesus with a difficult question.

"Master," he said, "what must I do so that I can live forever in God's kingdom?"

Jesus knew the lawyer wanted to trap him, so he asked him, "What does the law tell you about this?"

The lawyer answered, "I must love the Lord my God with all my heart and with all my soul and with all my strength, and I must love my neighbor as I love myself."

"That's right," said Jesus. "If you do that, you will live."

But the lawyer asked, "Who is my neighbor?"

Jesus answered with a parable.

"Once a man was going from Jerusalem to Jericho. The road was lonely and dangerous. A band of thieves suddenly sprang out and attacked the man. Then they left him half-dead by the roadside.

"For a long time, the man lay in the hot sun, too weak and injured to move, hoping desperately that someone would come and help him.

"At last he heard footsteps approaching.

"It was a priest. The man thought that surely a priest would help him. But the priest walked by without giving the man a second glance.

"A little while later, the injured man heard more footsteps. He opened his eyes and saw that a Levite, a servant of the Temple, was coming. The Levite came over and looked at him, but then walked on.

"Once again the man heard another traveler approaching. He painfully opened his eyes and saw that the traveler was a Samaritan. The man sank back with a groan. The Jews and Samaritans had been enemies for years. It was certainly no use expecting this Samaritan to help him. The man closed his eyes, all hope gone.

"But then the injured man felt gentle hands touching him. The Samaritan was bathing his wounds and bandaging his injuries.

"The Samaritan helped the injured man up and onto his donkey's back. Slowly and carefully, the Samaritan led the donkey along the stony road until they came to an inn.

"He led the man inside and took care of him, attending to his wounds once more and bringing him food and drink.

"When morning came, the Samaritan spoke to the innkeeper. 'Here are two pieces of silver,' he said. 'Take care of this man. If it costs more, I'll pay you the rest when I come back this way.'

"Now," said Jesus to the lawyer, "which one of those three was a neighbor to the man who was robbed and beaten?"

The lawyer answered, "The one who helped him."

And Jesus said, "Go and follow his example."

MATTHEW 18:12–14; LUKE 15:1–10

The Lost Sheep and the Lost Coin

The Pharisees and the scribes were muttering among themselves. "Just look at that! Jesus is talking to tax collectors and people who don't obey God's laws. He even eats with those people!"

Jesus heard them and told them this parable.

"Imagine a shepherd who has a hundred sheep. When he counts them one evening, he finds that only ninety-nine are safely in the fold. One of his sheep is lost. What does he do? He leaves the other ninety-nine sheep in a safe place and goes in search of the one that is missing.

"He searches all over the countryside and does not give up. When he finally finds his lost sheep, the shepherd is full of joy. He tenderly picks up the weary sheep and carries it home on his shoulders. Then he calls to his friends and neighbors and says, 'Look, be glad with me! I've found my sheep that was lost!'"

Jesus said, "I say to you that God is like this shepherd. There is more joy in heaven over one person who realizes that he has been doing wrong and changes his ways than over ninety-nine people who have been doing right all the time."

The Pharisees and scribes who were listening frowned and were not pleased with Jesus's words. Then Jesus told another parable to make his meaning clear.

"Imagine a woman who has ten pieces of silver. Suddenly she realizes that she has lost one of the coins. She is very upset because each coin is worth a great deal of money. Anxiously she lights the lamp and places it so that its light shines into every corner of her house. Then the woman gets her broom and sweeps carefully.

"She searches everywhere until at last she sees her coin, shining in the light of the lamp. She joyfully picks up her coin and calls to her friends and neighbors, 'Come here, let's celebrate! I lost my coin, but now I've found it. Be happy with me.'"

Jesus said to his listeners, "I tell you, there is joy among the angels over one sinner who repents."

LUKE 15:11–32

The Prodigal Son

Jesus told another parable for the benefit of the Pharisees and the scribes.

"There was once a man who had two sons. The older son was hardworking and obedient. But the younger son did not like being told what to do and was never content.

"The younger son knew his father was rich. He also knew that when his father died, everything would be divided between himself and his brother. But he did not want to wait for his father to die to enjoy himself.

"So, without thinking about his father's feelings at all, the younger son demanded, 'Give me my share now!'

"The father didn't want to force his son to stay by keeping him short of money. So he divided his estate between his two sons.

"As soon as the younger son received his share, he collected everything he owned and went off to a distant land.

"People soon found out that he had a lot of money, and they pretended to be his friends. For a while the young man enjoyed himself. But soon the money was gone, and so were his new 'friends.' To make things worse, there was a severe famine in the land.

"Now the young man was alone in a strange country with no money, no food, and no friends. He tried to get a job, but no one would employ him. Finally a man hired him to look after his pigs.

"One day as he sat watching the pigs, he thought about home. He realized that while he was starving to death, his father's servants had more than enough to eat.

"'I don't deserve to be called a son anymore,' he said to himself, 'but perhaps my father would make me one of his servants.'

"So the son set out on the long walk home. He wondered if his father would let him into the house at all.

"But as soon as the father saw him coming, he ran down the road to meet his son. The father threw his arms around him and called to the servants. 'Hurry, bring my son the finest clothes! Put a ring on his finger and kill the fattened calf we've been saving. We must celebrate! It was as if my son were dead, but now he's alive again!'

"When the elder son came in from the fields, he heard the music and laughter coming from the party. When he realized the reason for the celebration, he grew angry and refused to go inside the house.

"The father came hurrying out to him, because he loved both his sons. 'Come to the party!' he pleaded.

"The older son answered angrily. 'I've stayed here and worked hard for you all these years, and you've never even given me a young goat so I could have a party with my friends. But this son took half your money and wasted it. Then when he had nothing left, he came home, and you killed the best calf for a grand celebration!'

"'Son,' said his father, 'you have always been with me, and everything I have is yours! But we should still be glad and celebrate, because your brother was lost to us and now he's found.'"

Jesus explained that God is like the father in the story. He never stops loving us. God is ready to forgive anyone who is sorry for what he has done wrong. He is overjoyed when everything is well again.

JOHN 10; PSALM 23

Jesus as the Good Shepherd

Jesus moved steadily on toward Jerusalem. On the way, he explained more about himself to his disciples.

The disciples were used to seeing shepherds caring for their sheep. They knew that if danger from a lion or a bear threatened the flock, a good shepherd would die to protect his animals.

The disciples had seen shepherds searching for fresh pastures and cool streams for their flocks. They had seen shepherds searching for lost lambs and watching tenderly over the ewes. A good shepherd would know each animal individually.

So the disciples understood something of Jesus's love and care for them when he said, "I am the Good Shepherd. The Good Shepherd gives his life for his sheep. I am the Good Shepherd; I know my sheep, and they know me. As God the Father knows me, so I know the Father. And I lay down my life for the sheep.

"No man takes it from me. I lay it down myself. I have the power to lay it down, and I have the power to take it up. This is what I have been told to do by my Father."

Many people heard Jesus's words, and some of them grew angry.

"He is making himself out to be God!" they said.

The angry people wanted to stone him, but Jesus slipped away from them. He left Judea and went back across the River Jordan. Many of the people there believed in him. But he did not stay long.

Mary, Martha, and Lazarus

In the village of Bethany, about two miles from Jerusalem on the side of the Mount of Olives, there lived three friends of Jesus: Mary, Martha, and their brother Lazarus.

Martha had often invited Jesus to stay at their house. During one of his visits, she busied herself preparing the meal, trying to make everything nice for him.

Martha was becoming flustered and cross because her sister Mary wasn't helping at all. Mary was just sitting there, listening to Jesus.

For a while, Martha worked alone. Then words burst from her. "Lord, my sister is leaving me to do all the work! Don't you care? She should be helping me. You tell her!"

Jesus answered gently, "Martha, you're worrying about many things. But they're not really as important as what Mary has chosen to do. I won't take it from her."

Then Martha realized that listening to Jesus was more important than preparing special meals or being fussy about housework.

One day, as Jesus walked with his disciples, a man rushed up to him with a message from Mary and Martha.

"Your friend Lazarus is very ill," the man said urgently.

Jesus said quietly, "The end of this sickness is not death. God's glory will be shown because of it."

Though he loved his three friends very much, Jesus did not set off at once for Bethany. Instead, he remained where he was for two more days. Then he said to his disciples, "Let's go back to Judea."

The disciples were alarmed. Thomas was absolutely certain Jesus would be stoned to death if they went. Even so, he said, "Come on! Let's all go, so that we can die there with him."

By the time they neared Bethany, Lazarus had been buried for four days.

When Martha heard that Jesus was coming, she hurried out of the house to meet him. As soon as she reached him, she said, "Lord, if you'd been here, my brother wouldn't have died!"

Then she added, "But I know that God will do whatever you ask him, even now."

Jesus's eyes were full of sympathy and understanding. "Your brother will rise to life again," he said.

Martha faltered. "I know he will rise to life in the resurrection on the last day," she answered.

Quietly but clearly Jesus said, "I am the resurrection and the life. He who believes in me, though he were dead, yet will he live. And whoever lives and believes in me will never die. Do you believe this?"

Martha met his eyes. Quietly and calmly she replied, "Yes, Lord, I believe you are the Christ, the Son of God."

When she had said this, she slipped back to the house.

"Mary," she whispered, "Jesus wants to see you."

Mary stirred herself from her grief and hurried out to meet Jesus with her friends following her.

When Mary reached Jesus, she tearfully threw herself down at his feet. Mary used exactly the same words as Martha had.

"Lord, if you'd been here, my brother wouldn't have died!"

When Jesus saw how she wept and that her friends wept also, he was distressed. "Where have you buried Lazarus?" he asked.

"Come and see," they answered.

When Jesus reached the tomb, he said, "Take away the stone."

There was a pause. Then Martha said, "Lord, by now the body will smell. Lazarus has been dead for four days."

Jesus answered her, "Didn't I say that if you believed, you would see God's glory?"

So, hesitantly at first, the people moved the stone away.

Jesus then prayed to God. When he finished his prayer, he called out loudly, "Lazarus, come out here!"

And the man who had been dead came out. His body was still wrapped in grave clothes, and his face was still covered by a cloth.

"Help him remove those grave clothes," Jesus said.

The people did as Jesus told them to do.

Many of the Jews then believed that Jesus was indeed the Messiah, the Son of God. But others of them went to the chief priests and the Pharisees and reported these events to them.

"He's got to be stopped!" said the chief priests and the Pharisees. And from that day on, they plotted to kill Jesus.

So Jesus went secretly to the village of Ephraim and stayed there until the time was right for what he knew must happen.

MATTHEW 21:1–17; 26:3–5; MARK 11:1–11, 15–19; LUKE 19:28–40, 45–48; JOHN 11:55–57; 12:12–19

Palm Sunday

It was nearly time for the Festival of the Passover. Many people were traveling to Jerusalem to join in the celebration. The favorite topic of most conversations was speculation about Jesus.

"Do you think Jesus will come?" they would ask each other. "Probably not. He must know about the order from the Pharisees and the chief priests that anyone who knows where Jesus is must report him. They are waiting for the right moment to arrest him."

Jesus did indeed know of the order. But it did not change his mind. He set out from Ephraim with his disciples.

As they neared Bethphage, a village on the Mount of Olives, he said to two of his disciples, "Go into the village. You'll see a donkey tied up there. She'll have a young colt beside her which no one has ridden yet. Bring the colt here to me."

Jesus went on, "If anyone asks you what you're doing, just say, 'The Lord needs the colt and will send it back again soon.'"

The disciples were puzzled. Why did Jesus need a donkey's colt?

Later they remembered the words of the prophets. The prophets foretold that the king of the Jews would come to his people humbly, riding on the colt of a donkey.

But now they went into Bethphage to get the colt.

When they returned, Jesus was waiting for them. The disciples realized he was going to ride the colt, so they spread their garments on its back to make a saddle.

Word spread quickly, and a crowd gathered near the road.

"Jesus is coming!" they cried.

People threw their garments down in the road so that Jesus might ride over them. Some people spread branches cut from palm trees on the road. Others waved the branches like banners.

People were shouting, "Hosanna to the Son of David! Blessed is he that comes in the name of the Lord! Hosanna in the highest!"

Jesus and his followers entered the streets of Jerusalem, and Jesus went directly to the Temple.

When Jesus saw what was happening at the Temple, anger rose within him.

The Temple looked like a marketplace. Lambs, young goats, doves, and pigeons trembled in cages, waiting to be bought and used as sacrifices.

There were moneychangers as well. Because Roman coins could not be used in the Temple, men sat at tables with piles of coins, ready to make change for the people who wanted to buy sacrifices.

As Jesus watched, he saw that the moneychangers were making a profit. They were lining their pockets with money the people were bringing to give to God.

Jesus was furious. He picked up a piece of rope which lay on the ground nearby and slammed it down like a whip, scattering coins everywhere. Jesus overturned all the tables and freed the animals.

Then Jesus looked at the animal sellers and the moneychangers and said, "It is written in the Scriptures, 'My house shall be called a house of prayer.' But you have made it a den of thieves!"

The disciples stood and watched, unable to move. Jesus, their beloved Lord, was already in danger of death. Instead of appeasing the chief priests and the Pharisees, he was making them even angrier.

The blind and lame people came to Jesus, begging to be healed. And Jesus healed them, right there in the Temple.

The Temple was filled with confusion and noise. But above all the uproar, some of the children who had been following Jesus could still be heard shouting, "Hosanna! Hosanna to the Son of David!"

The Pharisees could no longer suppress their anger.

"Don't you hear what they're saying?" they demanded.

"Certainly I hear them," Jesus replied. "Haven't you read the Scriptures where this was foretold? 'Out of the mouths of babies and children you shall hear perfect praise.'"

Again Jesus was correcting them, the experts on the Scripture. He continued, "If the people hadn't called out, even the stones would have taken up the cry."

Even though the chief priests and Pharisees had Jesus in their grasp, they dared not touch him. They were afraid that the crowd would turn against them. "It's no use," they said. "Next he'll be leading the people to revolt. He must be stopped. We'll have to capture him secretly."

It was getting late in the day. Jesus took his twelve disciples and went to the village of Bethany for the night.

211

Supper at Bethany

One evening when Jesus and his disciples were in Bethany, Simon, who had been a leper, invited them to supper at his house.

As the guests reclined at the table, a woman came into the room. In her hands she held an alabaster jar of precious perfume.

Quietly the woman went over to Jesus. Gently and reverently she poured the perfume over his head and his feet. Then she dried his feet with her hair.

The lovely scent of the perfume filled the room. The guests looked at her silently and were puzzled.

Then Judas Iscariot, who was in charge of the disciples' money, spoke sharply. "What a waste," he said. "That perfume could have been sold, and the money given to the poor."

Some of the other disciples agreed. The woman shrank back. She had tried to tell Jesus that she knew of the sorrow and suffering that was to come to him and that she cared deeply. But her action of love had been misunderstood. She'd been stupid and wasteful.

But Jesus had not misunderstood.

"Leave her alone!" he said. "What she has done is beautiful. There will always be poor people among you whom you can help. But you will not always have me. She poured this perfume over me to prepare my body for the burial which is to come. And I tell you that wherever the Gospel is preached throughout the whole world, her love revealed here will also be told. Her action will never be forgotten."

The woman knew Jesus understood her as he protected her from the disciples' harsh words. And she loved him more than ever.

But Judas was furious. In his anger and disappointment, Judas went secretly to the chief priests and officers of the Temple.

"I know where Jesus is," he told them. "I will tell you where he goes, and you will be able to capture him in a quiet place away from the sight of the crowds."

The chief priests rubbed their hands together in delight. They thought they were going to be rid of Jesus at last.

They promised Judas Iscariot thirty pieces of silver as a reward. Judas began watching for a chance to hand Jesus over to them.

The Widow in the Temple

When Jesus and his disciples reached Jerusalem, they went straight to the Temple. As usual, a large crowd gathered eagerly to hear Jesus's teaching.

"Beware of the teachers of the law," he warned them. "They walk around full of their own importance. They have places reserved for them in the synagogues, and they sit in the best seats at the feasts. But secretly they cheat the poor and take away their homes. Then they stand where everyone can see them and recite long prayers, so that people will be impressed by how good they are. But God is not deceived. The lawyers will be punished for their deeds."

As the disciples listened, they were afraid for Jesus, for this kind of teaching would anger the authorities still more. Yet the disciples understood that Jesus couldn't bear to see the people betrayed by the very men who should be showing them the love of God.

Now as Jesus sat there, he could see people putting money into the offering box. Many rich men came swaggering through the crowds. They dropped their silver and gold coins into the box with a loud clatter, hoping to impress everyone with the amount they had given.

Then a woman whose husband had died came into the Temple. It was clear that she was very poor. She was pale and shabbily dressed. Hoping no one would notice her, she quietly dropped two small copper coins into the offering box.

As she moved away, she was ashamed because her offering was so small. Jesus spoke to the listening crowd. "I tell you that this poor widow has given more than any of those rich people gave."

The crowd gaped at him. How could he say that? Hadn't he seen the two tiny coins?

Jesus explained. "The rich men gave out of their plenty. It was such a small proportion of their wealth that they won't even notice it has gone. But this woman has given God all the money she had, because she loves him. She gave her all. No one can ever give more than that."

Now the crowd understood. The widow hurried away, but there was a warm glow in her heart.

Judas stood back and watched. He was still waiting for a chance to betray Jesus.

The Last Supper

It was the first day of the Festival of the Passover. Jesus's disciples
asked him, "Where shall we eat the Passover meal?" They were
wondering if there was a safe place anywhere in Jerusalem.

Jesus took Peter and John to one side. "Go into Jerusalem," he
said. "As you enter the city, you will meet a man carrying a pitcher of
water. He will lead you to a house. Say to the owner of the house,
'The Teacher asks where he may eat the Passover meal with his
disciples.' He will show you to a large upper room. That is where you
must make everything ready."

Peter and John did as Jesus said and were led to the upper room.
There they made the preparations for the Passover meal. Then they
returned to Jesus and the others. Later that evening, the twelve
disciples went with Jesus to the upper room.

In that hot, dusty country, it was the custom for a servant to wash
the feet of anyone coming into a house. But the disciples went
straight to the table. None of them intended to be a servant to the
others.

So as the meal was being served, Jesus stood up, poured water
into a basin, and washed their feet.

The disciples watched, first in amazement, then with shame.

When Jesus had washed all the disciples' feet, he sat once more at
the table.

"Do you understand?" he asked. "Because I, your Lord and
Teacher, have washed your feet, you should be ready to wash one
another's feet. I did this so that you could copy me. Don't be
ashamed to carry out such tasks. If you serve one another, you will be
happy and blessed. And whoever is kind to any messenger of mine is
being kind to me and to the one who sent me."

Now they were ready to start their meal.

It was their last supper together. Jesus was very troubled. "I tell you truly," he said, "one of you here will betray me."

Only Judas knew exactly what he meant. Judas had already secretly agreed to betray Jesus to the Jewish authorities. But the other disciples were not aware of this. They were upset, fearing that they might indeed betray Jesus in a moment of carelessness or doubt.

John was sitting next to Jesus. "Lord," he pleaded in a low voice, "who is it?"

Jesus answered, "It is he to whom I give this bread."

He dipped some bread into the sauce and handed it to Judas.

Judas met Jesus's eyes and tried to bluff his way out. "Surely you don't mean me!" he said.

But Jesus knew. "Go and do what you have to do," he replied.

Judas got up and went out into the night.

None of the other disciples realized what was happening. They knew Judas was in charge of the money. So they thought Jesus had told him to go and buy something they needed.

During the meal Jesus took the bread and gave thanks to God for it. Then he broke the bread and gave it to the eleven, saying, "Eat this. It is my body, broken for you. Do this in memory of me."

Then Jesus took the wine, and when he had given thanks to God, he poured the wine for the disciples. He said, "Drink all of it. This is the cup of the New Covenant in my blood which is shed for you. I will drink no more of the fruit of the vine until the day I drink it once again in the Kingdom of God."

The disciples were puzzled and distressed.

"God's glory will be revealed," Jesus said. "My beloved friends, I shall not be with you much longer. So I give you a new commandment. Love one another as I have loved you."

"Lord, where are you going?" they asked. "We will come with you. We would die for you!"

"All of you will desert me and run away," said Jesus. "And Peter, before the rooster crows today, you will say three times that you never knew me."

"I'll never deny knowing you!" Peter cried, deeply distressed.

Jesus continued to comfort his special group of friends. "Don't let your hearts be troubled! You believe in God, so believe in me also. In my Father's house, there are many rooms. I go to prepare a place for you. And I will come again and take you there. You know where I am going, and you know the way."

Thomas said, "Lord, we don't know where you are going, so how can we know the way?"

Jesus answered, "I am the way, the truth, and the life. No one comes to the Father, except by me."

He looked around at their troubled faces. "If you love me, obey my words. I will ask the Father to send you another comforter, who will be able to stay with you forever. Soon the world shall see me no more. But you will see me. And because I live, you will live also. Peace I leave with you; my peace I give to you. Do not let your heart be troubled, neither let it be afraid."

After Jesus and the disciples had talked a while longer, they sang a hymn and went out into the night.

They walked in the darkness until they came to the Garden of Gethsemane.

And Judas knew exactly where they had gone.

MATTHEW 26:36–75; 27:1–26; MARK 14:32–72; 15:1–15; LUKE 22:39–71; 23:1–25; JOHN 18:3–40; 19:1–16

The Trials of Jesus

The Garden of Gethsemane was dark and shadowy in the moonlight. Jesus said to his disciples, "Sit here while I go over there and pray. Peter, James, and John, come a little further with me."

"Keep watch," said Jesus to the three disciples. "My sorrow is so great—it almost crushes me."

Jesus went a little way apart from them and knelt on the ground. He prayed, "Father, if it is your will, take this cup of suffering from me. But let your will be done, not mine."

Then Jesus came back to Peter, James, and John. Instead of keeping watch as he had asked, they had fallen asleep.

Jesus said, "Couldn't you keep watch for just one hour?"

The three disciples woke up, very ashamed.

Twice more Jesus asked the disciples to keep watch, and twice more he returned to find them sleeping. The last time he said, "Look, the hour has come. Here comes the one who will betray me."

The disciples looked and saw a crowd approaching, carrying sticks and swords.

Jesus stepped forward calmly and quietly, facing the rabble.

Judas pushed his way to the front. He went to Jesus, kissed him, and called him "Rabbi," for this was the secret sign that had been arranged with the chief priests.

"Do you betray the Son of Man with a kiss?" Jesus asked him.

Soldiers moved forward to arrest Jesus. Peter was furious and seized a sword, cutting off the ear of the servant of Caiaphas, the high priest.

But Jesus touched the man's ear and healed him.

"Put down your swords," he said to his followers. "For he who lives by the sword shall die by the sword. Don't you think I could ask my Father for help? He could send legions of angels to defend me. But if I do, the scriptures will not be fulfilled. Do you think I will not obey my Father's will?"

Jesus spoke to the crowd. "Am I leading a revolt? Is that why you come to capture me with sticks and swords? Didn't you see me every day, teaching in the Temple? You didn't arrest me then."

Finally, he said to the soldiers, "I am Jesus of Nazareth whom you have come to arrest. Let these others go."

His disciples, seeing what was going to happen next, deserted Jesus and fled.

Jesus was bound and led away. Peter and John couldn't bear not knowing what was happening. So they stopped running and turned to follow Jesus. They kept well back and remained hidden in the darkness.

Jesus was taken before Caiaphas, the high priest, to be put on trial by the Sanhedrin, the Jewish high court.

Peter and John waited outside in the courtyard. Peter watched as people were being taken inside to tell lies about Jesus. The chief priests were determined to have Jesus killed.

Jesus listened to the many lies, but he remained silent until Caiaphas spoke. "Tell us. Are you the Son of God?"

Jesus answered, "Yes, as you have said. And you will see the Son of Man sitting at the right hand of God and coming in the clouds of heaven."

"He speaks blasphemy!" announced Caiaphas.

"He must be put to death!" shouted the chief priests and the elders. Then they began to strike Jesus.

Outside, Peter heard the shouts. Then one of the maids noticed him. "You!" she said. "You were with that man."

"No!" Peter said in fear, and he hastily walked away.

Another girl saw him and said, "You were with Jesus."

"I don't know what you're talking about!" protested Peter.

But later other people said, "You are one of them. We can tell you come from Galilee by the way you talk."

Peter was desperate. "I tell you *I don't know him!*" he shouted. And then as the people looked at him with hard, unfriendly eyes, Peter heard a rooster crow.

He remembered what Jesus had said to him. "Before the rooster crows today, you will say three times that you never knew me."

Peter rushed outside and cried bitterly in shame and sorrow.

It was dawn. The chief priests and the elders took Jesus under guard to Pilate, the Roman governor of that district.

Judas saw this. He realized Jesus had been condemned to death by the Jews, and he couldn't bear it. He took the thirty pieces of silver which had been his reward for betraying Jesus and hurried to the chief priests and elders. He threw the money back at them. Then, unable to live with what he had done to Jesus, he hanged himself.

Now Jesus stood silently while Pilate questioned him. Then Pilate asked, "Are you king of the Jews?"

"You say that I am," said Jesus.

The chief priests and elders accused him of many things, but Jesus answered not one word.

Stirred up by the Jewish leaders, a crowd of people had collected. "I can't find anything with which to charge this man," Pilate said. "I'll have him whipped, and then I'll let him go."

But the crowd shouted, "No, no, free Barabbas instead!"

Pilate knew that at this feast, one prisoner was always released. He had hoped to release Jesus. But the crowd howled for Barabbas, a murderer. Pilate didn't want a riot to start.

He tried once more to save Jesus. "Which of the two do you want me to free? Jesus or Barabbas?"

"Barabbas!" they yelled.

"Then what shall I do with Jesus?" asked Pilate.

"Crucify him!" they yelled.

Pilate sent for a basin of water. In front of them all, he washed his hands as a sign that he wasn't making the decision.

"This is your responsibility," he declared.

So Barabbas was freed, and Jesus was whipped. Then he was handed over to be crucified.

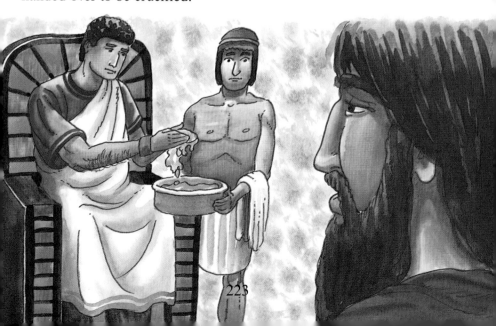

The Crucifixion

The Roman soldiers stripped Jesus of his clothes. They dressed him in a purple robe and put a crown of thorns on his head. Then they put a staff in his hand and cruelly made fun of him by kneeling down and saying, "Hail, king of the Jews!"

The soldiers took the staff and struck him with it.

Jesus's own clothes were put on him again. Then he was forced to carry a heavy cross to the place called Golgotha.

Weakened by the beatings, Jesus fainted on the way up the hill. A man named Simon of Cyrene was forced to carry the cross for Jesus.

At the place of execution, the soldiers nailed Jesus to the cross with one nail through each hand and foot.

The hammer blows fell. Jesus was in great pain, but he prayed to God, "Father, forgive them, for they know not what they do."

The cross was lifted and set into place. Then the soldiers sat down and began to divide up Jesus's clothes among them. They threw dice to see who would win his robe.

Two thieves were crucified on either side of Jesus. One thief was sorry for the wrong he had done and asked Jesus to think of him. To him Jesus said, "Today you will be with me in paradise."

As Jesus looked down from the cross, he saw his mother, Mary, and his disciple John. He said, "Woman, here is your son. Son, here is your mother." They realized that Jesus wanted them to be as mother and son to one another and to comfort each other.

Now Jesus was in very great pain. He called out to God, fulfilling the prophecy of the psalmist, "My God, my God, why have you forsaken me?"

After a while he said, "I am thirsty." So the people below soaked a sponge in vinegar and held it up to his lips.

Soon Jesus said, "It is finished. Father, into your hands I commit my spirit." And he died.

For the last three hours that Jesus was on the cross, there was darkness over all the land. As he died, there was a great earthquake, and the curtain which hung in the Temple was ripped in two.

The people were very afraid. The Roman soldiers who had helped crucify him were terrified. When they saw these things, they said, "Surely, this was the Son of God."

Jesus and the two thieves were crucified on Friday. The next day was the Jewish Sabbath, so that Friday afternoon, the Jewish rulers asked Pilate that the bodies be taken down. They did not wish them to be hanging there on a holy day.

First the soldiers broke the legs of the two thieves so that they died at once. But when they went to break the legs of Jesus, they found he was already dead. So as the Scriptures had foretold, none of his bones were broken. To be certain of his death, one of the soldiers pierced Jesus's side with a spear.

Joseph from Arimathea was a wealthy member of the Sanhedrin who had secretly believed in Jesus. He went boldly to Pilate and asked for the body of Jesus. He wanted to bury it properly.

Pilate gave Joseph permission to bury Jesus.

Joseph and Nicodemus, another secret follower of Jesus, went to Golgotha. They took Jesus's body and wrapped it with spices in a new linen cloth, as was the burial custom of the Jews.

Then they placed Jesus's body in the tomb which Joseph had intended to be his own when he died. The new tomb, which had been freshly cut out of solid rock, was in a garden close to the place where Jesus had been crucified. Joseph then rolled a large stone across the tomb to close it.

The women who had been with Jesus at the cross took note of the location of the tomb.

It was now the Sabbath, and the chief priests and the Pharisees went to Pilate because they were still anxious.

"Sir," they said, "we remember that while this liar was still alive he said, 'In three days, I will be raised from the dead.' Command that a guard watch over the tomb until the third day has passed. Otherwise his disciples may steal the body and say that he is alive."

"Very well," said Pilate. "Make the tomb as secure as possible."

So the chief priests and the Pharisees went to the garden, taking Roman soldiers with them. They put a seal on the stone so that it would be impossible to move it without the seal being broken. They also left well-drilled and highly disciplined Roman soldiers on guard.

Then they left the tomb believing that they were finished with Jesus and his teaching for good.

The Resurrection

At sunrise on Sunday morning, a violent earthquake shook the ground. In the garden where Jesus was buried, an angel of the Lord came down, rolled the stone away from the tomb, and sat on it. The angel's appearance was like a flash of lightning. When the Roman guards saw him, they fainted in terror.

Mary Magdalene and some of the other women were on their way to the tomb, taking more spices with them to anoint the body of Jesus.

By the time they arrived, the angel had gone and the soldiers had awakened and fled in fear. Mary Magdalene hastened along in front of the others and saw that the stone had been rolled away. In great distress, she ran back to find Peter and John.

The other women arrived at the tomb. Fearfully they crept inside and gazed around. But the body of Jesus was no longer there. Suddenly two angels in shining white clothes stood beside them.

"You are looking for Jesus, who was crucified," said the angels. "But why are you looking for the living among the dead? He is not here. He is risen! Remember what he told you.

"Now, go and give this message to the disciples. Tell them that Jesus is going before you into Galilee, and you will see him there."

The women ran as fast as they could to deliver the news.

But Mary Magdalene had already reached Peter and John. "They have taken him away!" she sobbed. "And we don't know what they've done with his body!"

Stricken with fear and grief, Peter and John ran to the tomb. John arrived first and paused at the entrance. Peering in, he saw the cloths that had been used to wrap the body of Jesus.

Then Peter arrived and went straight into the tomb.

Peter saw the linen cloth and wrappings which had bound Jesus's head. The cloths were lying separately and were neatly folded.

And Peter believed.

Then John also entered the tomb. He and Peter looked at each other in amazement. Puzzled and not fully understanding, they returned to the house where the other disciples were waiting.

Now Mary Magdalene stumbled forward and looked into the tomb. There she saw two angels sitting where the body of Jesus had been laid—one at the foot and the other at the head. But Mary did not realize they were angels.

"Woman, why are you crying?" they asked.

"Because they have taken away my Lord," she sobbed.

Mary then turned around and saw someone standing there. Blinded by her tears, she did not recognize him.

"Woman, why are you weeping?" the person asked. "Who is it that you are looking for?"

Mary thought he must be the gardener. "Sir, if you took him away, please tell me where you have put him!" she begged.

Then Jesus said, "Mary."

She turned fully toward him and cried, "Rabboni!" which means

"Teacher."

"Go to my friends," Jesus said. "Tell them I am returning to my Father. I am returning to God."

Mary was overjoyed and hurried back to the group of disciples. "I have seen the Lord!" she cried. Then she gave them his message.

But the disciples couldn't believe he had risen.

Late that same Sunday evening, the disciples were gathered in the room of a house. All the doors were locked tightly because they were afraid that the Jewish authorities would find them and arrest them.

Suddenly Jesus was standing in the room among them.

"Peace be with you!" he greeted them. The disciples gazed at him in fear, thinking he was a ghost. He held out his hands so that they could see the marks left by the nails. Then Jesus showed them where his side had been pierced by the Roman soldier's spear.

At last the disciples could accept the truth.

Thomas, who was not there when Jesus appeared to the disciples, returned some time later. The disciples excitedly told him the news.

But Thomas shook his head. "Unless I can see and touch the marks of the nails and the wound in his side, I won't believe!" he said.

And Thomas continued to grieve deeply.

The Roman Guards Talk to the Chief Priests

Some of the guards who had been at the tomb when the stone was rolled away went to the chief priests. They told them everything that had happened.

The chief priests went to the other Jewish leaders. They decided that the guards' story could not be allowed to spread.

Together the Jewish leaders worked out a plan.

"Listen," they said to the guards, "you must say that Jesus's disciples came in the night and stole his body while you were asleep."

Then they offered the soldiers a large sum of money as a bribe.

The guards took the bribe and spread a false story. Many of the Jews believed it.

But more of Jesus's disciples were beginning to learn the truth.

The Walk to Emmaus and Thomas Is Convinced

That Sunday evening, two of Jesus's followers were walking sadly to Emmaus from Jerusalem. Jesus drew near and walked alongside them.

Buried in their grief, the two didn't recognize Jesus. As they traveled together, Jesus asked them why they were so unhappy.

One of the men, Cleopas, said, "How can you not know about Jesus of Nazareth?" said Cleopas. "He was a powerful prophet, but the chief priests and rulers demanded that he be crucified. Now some of our women say that angels have told them that Jesus is alive."

Jesus answered, "You are so slow to believe. It was necessary that all those things should happen."

Then Jesus began to explain the prophecies about the Messiah, beginning with the books of Moses.

When they reached Emmaus, Jesus said he was going to walk farther. But Cleopas said, "It's getting late. Spend the night here."

So Jesus went into the house with them. When the meal was ready, Jesus took the bread and blessed it. Then he broke the bread and handed it to them. There was something familiar in the way he did this.

They recognized him immediately. In that moment, he disappeared from their sight. The two men rushed all the way back to Jerusalem to tell the other disciples.

But it was seven more days before Thomas was convinced.

Once again the disciples were in the room with the doors shut and locked. It was just as before, but this time Thomas was present with the others. Suddenly Jesus was there with them.

Gently he spoke to Thomas. "Put your finger in the marks of the nails and your hand into the wound in my side. And believe."

But Thomas did not need to touch the nail prints nor put his hand into the wound. Filled with a mixture of awe, love, and almost overwhelming joy, he whispered reverently, "My Lord and my God."

Jesus said, "You believe because you see me. Blessed are those who have not seen me and yet have believed."

MATTHEW 28:16–20; JOHN 21:1–20

Breakfast on the Shore

Jesus had said that he would go before his disciples into Galilee. Now seven of the twelve waited there for him near the shores of the Sea of Galilee. Peter was one of the seven. He longed to see Jesus again; yet he was very upset about having denied knowing him three times.

After a while Peter said, "I'm going fishing."

"We'll come with you," said the others. Anything was better than this waiting.

So they got into a boat and cast off. All night they fished, but they caught nothing. Dejectedly they began to sail toward the shore.

The sun had just begun to rise as the boat approached the land. The disciples could see a man standing on the beach.

The man called to them, "Have you caught any fish, my children?"

"No," they answered.

He said, "Throw your net on the right side of the boat."

Once before, someone had told them to do that. The disciples let the net down, and immediately it was so full of fish that they couldn't haul it in. "It is Jesus!" John said.

When they landed on the beach, a fire was already burning with fish cooking on it. There was bread waiting for them as well.

"Come and have breakfast," Jesus invited them.

When the meal was over, Jesus said, "Simon Peter, do you love me?"

"Yes, Lord," Peter replied. "You know I love you."

Three times Jesus asked Peter this question, and three times Peter said yes. Jesus then said, "Care for my sheep."

Now Peter knew that he had been forgiven for those three times that he had declared he didn't know Jesus. And what was even more wonderful, Jesus had commanded Peter to care for his followers.

Some days later, the other disciples were also entrusted with the task of continuing Jesus's work on earth. They gathered on a mountain in Galilee, as Jesus had instructed them to do. When he appeared to them there, they worshiped him, although some of them doubted it was really Jesus. Then he came closer and spoke to them.

"All authority in heaven and on earth is given to me," he said. "Go and make disciples everywhere, baptizing them in name of the Father and of the Son and of the Holy Spirit.

"Teach them to obey all the commands I have given you. And lo, I am with you always, even to the end of the world."

LUKE 24:49–51; ACTS 1:3–12

The Ascension

For forty days after his crucifixion, Jesus appeared at different times
to his disciples. Some of his followers had doubted, but by now the
eleven were absolutely convinced of the truth of his resurrection.

As they ate their last meal together, Jesus said to them, "You must
wait here in Jerusalem for the gift which my Father will send to
you—the gift of the Holy Spirit."

Jesus knew he could no longer remain on earth with the disciples.
He led them outside the city to the Mount of Olives.

"When the Holy Spirit comes to you, you will receive power," he
promised them. "You will speak of me in Jerusalem, in all Judea and
Samaria, and to the end of the earth."

He lifted up his hands to bless them, and even as he did so, he
was taken up from them and received into the skies. Then a cloud hid
him so that they could no longer see him.

As the disciples gazed upward, two men dressed in shining white
garments appeared and spoke to them.

"Men of Galilee, why do you stand gazing upward into the sky?
This Jesus, whom you have seen taken up into heaven, will one day
return in the same manner."

Filled with joy, the disciples went back to Jerusalem.

ACTS 1:26; 2
The Gift of the Holy Spirit

Fifty days after the Feast of the Passover came the Feast of Pentecost. Only ten days earlier, Jesus had ascended into heaven. The disciples were still waiting for the gift of the Holy Spirit which Jesus had promised to them.

They chose Matthias to be one of the twelve in place of Judas Iscariot, and they became known as the apostles. On the day of Pentecost, they gathered together in the room of a house in Jerusalem.

Suddenly there came a sound from heaven like a rushing, mighty wind. It filled the whole house. As the apostles looked at each other in fear, they saw what seemed to be tongues of fire. The fire divided so that a flame rested above each one of them.

The apostles were filled with the Holy Spirit of God, just as Jesus had promised them.

As they spoke to each other, they found that they were talking in different languages, guided by the power of the Holy Spirit.

Jews from many nations were staying in Jerusalem to worship God at the Feast of Pentecost. When the news about the apostles spread, a crowd of these people came to listen. The visiting Jews were utterly amazed, because each one of them heard the apostles speaking in his own language—languages which the apostles had never spoken before.

Some of the listening crowd began to laugh and jeered, "They're drunk! That's what it is."

But Peter stood up boldly in front of them all, and the other apostles stood with him.

"Listen to me," said Peter. "These men aren't drunk."

Then he told them how the Scriptures said that God's Holy Spirit would be poured out on men, that their sons and daughters would prophesy, and that their old men would dream dreams. Then Peter told them the story of Jesus.

Around three thousand people heard, believed, and were baptized. Many miraculous signs and wonders were performed.

Now all of the believers shared everything they had. They met every day in the Temple and in each other's homes. They ate together, prayed together, and learned together.

They were happy and they praised God. Each day, more and more people believed.

But the authorities were watching.

The Lame Man at the Beautiful Gate

In Jerusalem there lived a man who was unable to walk because he had been born lame. Because there was no work he could do, he was forced to beg for money.

Every day he was carried to the gate which was called Beautiful. Many people passed him on their way to and from the Temple, and often they gave him money.

One afternoon the lame man saw Peter and John coming toward him. "Please!" he called out. "Give me whatever you can spare!"

Then Peter spoke. "I don't have any silver or gold," he said, "but I will give you what I do have. In the name of Jesus Christ of Nazareth, get up and walk!"

Then Peter stretched out a hand to the man. Bravely he clasped

Peter's hand and struggled to stand. He then took a few steps, testing his new ability. He could walk!

Peter and John went on into the Temple, and the man went with them, walking, leaping, and praising God.

People already in the Temple saw him, and they were amazed.

Then Peter told the people about Jesus, and they listened.

The priests, the Sadducees, and the captain of the temple guard were furious. They had Peter and John thrown into prison.

The next morning Peter and John were brought from prison and put on trial before the Sanhedrin, the Jewish court.

"Tell us, by what power did you heal this man?" they asked.

Then Peter was filled with the power of the Holy Spirit and replied without hesitation, "It was by the power of Jesus Christ. He is the only one with the power to save."

The council members were amazed. Peter and John were just ordinary men. Yet they spoke with such boldness and courage. Truly these men had been with Jesus.

"In the future, you are not to speak or teach in the name of Jesus," ordered Caiaphas, the high priest who had tried Jesus.

Courageously, Peter and John replied, "Decide for yourselves if it is right for us to obey you instead of God. We must tell everyone of the miraculous things we have seen and heard."

The council members became even more furious, and they made many threats against Peter and John. But in the end, the two apostles were released. As before, the Jewish leaders were afraid to act because of the people.

Peter and John went back to the house where they were staying. Soberly they told the others what had happened.

Then all the believers there joined together in prayer. They prayed for God to give them boldness so that they could continue to preach his message unafraid.

After they had prayed, they were filled with the power of the Holy Spirit, and they were not afraid to speak God's message.

Stephen

The number of believers was growing every day. They were still trying to share everything, but some of them had begun to grumble over the way things were distributed.

So the believers chose seven men to take over the task of distributing things.

Among the seven was Stephen, a man full of faith and the Holy Spirit. He was a great preacher and also performed many miracles.

The Jewish leaders were frightened. This new gospel of Christ was spreading too far and too fast.

When Stephen started to preach, certain members of the synagogue were among the crowd listening to him. They argued with him. But Stephen was filled with the Holy Spirit and wisely avoided their traps.

Then the members of the synagogue bribed men to tell lies about Stephen. They had him brought before the Sanhedrin, where they continued their false accusations.

"What do you have to say to these charges?" the high priest asked him angrily.

Stephen replied fully, beginning with the lives of Abraham and Moses and finishing with an accusation against the Jews themselves. "You are all the same," he said. "Your fathers killed the prophets of the Christ, and now you have murdered the Christ himself."

His listeners were so furious that they could not contain themselves. But Stephen looked upward. "I see the heavens opened and the Son of Man standing at the right hand of God!" he said.

The people in the court put their hands over their ears, so they could not hear any more. Screaming and shouting, they dragged Stephen out of the city and began to stone him.

Some of the men who had falsely accused Stephen now slipped off their outer robes, so they could throw better. They laid their robes at the feet of a young man named Saul.

As the stones rained down on him, Stephen prayed openly, "Lord Jesus, receive my spirit." When he could no longer stand, he fell to his knees and cried out, "Lord, do not hold this sin against them."

So Stephen died. And Saul watched with approval.

That same day a great persecution began against all the believers in Jerusalem, and many of them fled.

Saul was determined to destroy all the believers. He searched for them from home to home in Jerusalem, dragging any believers that he found off to prison.

The believers who had fled were now scattered throughout Judea and Samaria. But wherever they went, they preached about Jesus. So the gospel of the Kingdom of God began to spread.

Philip, one of the seven selected by the believers, went to the city of Samaria and began to preach about Jesus there.

Acts 8:5–8, 26–40; 9:1

Philip and the Ethiopian

Crowds came to listen to Philip as he preached in Samaria, and he healed many sick people. There was much happiness in the city.

Then one day an angel appeared to him with a message from God. "Philip, you must go south to the desert road that goes from Jerusalem to Gaza."

Leave the city where things were going so well and travel to a desert road which practically no one used?

But Philip obeyed. After he reached his destination, Philip stood at the roadside. Why had God sent him there?

Then in the distance, he saw a chariot. It was coming toward him from Jerusalem and would soon pass the spot where he was standing.

The Holy Spirit spoke to Philip. "Go across to that chariot and stay close to it."

So as the chariot passed, Philip caught up with it and ran alongside. He saw that inside the chariot sat a man from the country of Ethiopia.

To Philip's surprise, the Ethiopian was reading aloud from the book of Isaiah, part of the Scriptures. He had come to the words, "He was led as a sheep to the slaughter; and like a lamb silent before his shearer, so he opened not his mouth."

Panting, Philip called out to the man, "Do you understand what you are reading?"

Startled, the Ethiopian looked up and saw Philip. "How can I understand if no one explains it to me?" he asked.

"I can explain," said Philip.

The Ethiopian stopped the chariot, and Philip climbed in.

As the chariot drove on, the Ethiopian explained that he had been to Jerusalem to worship God, and now he was on his way home.

The Ethiopian turned back to the words of Isaiah. "Who is the writer talking about?" he asked. "Does he mean that he is the sheep led to the slaughter? Or is he speaking of someone else?"

Then Philip told him the story of Jesus. The Ethiopian listened closely, and as he listened, he believed.

As they passed beside some water along the roadside, the Ethiopian cried out, "Look! Can I be baptized here at once?"

Philip nodded. "If you believe with all your heart, you may."

The Ethiopian ordered his driver to stop. Philip and the Ethiopian climbed down to the dusty road. Then they both went into the water, and Philip baptized the Ethiopian.

When they came out of the water, the Holy Spirit suddenly took Philip away. His work in that place was finished. Rejoicing, the Ethiopian continued happily on his journey home.

Philip found himself at Azotus and journeyed on to Caesarea, preaching as he went.

But back in Jerusalem, Saul was still violently persecuting the believers.

ACTS 9:1–31

Saul

Saul wasn't satisfied with persecuting only the believers in Jerusalem. So he set out for Damascus to wipe out Jesus's followers there.

But as he traveled along the road to the city of Damascus, Saul was suddenly surrounded by a light of unearthly brilliance.

Saul fell to the ground. He heard a voice speaking to him. "Saul, Saul, why do you persecute me?"

Trembling, he whispered, "Who are you, Lord?"

The answer came. "I am Jesus, whom you are persecuting. Get up and go into Damascus. There you will receive your instructions."

The men who were traveling with Saul stood silent and fearful. They heard the voice, but they did not see anyone.

Saul stumbled to his feet. He put a hand to his eyes. He couldn't see! He was blind.

One of the men took Saul's hand. "Come," he said. "We'll lead you the rest of the way to Damascus."

They took Saul to the house of Judas. For three days he could not see. During that time he refused to eat or drink. But Saul did pray.

Living in Damascus was a believer named Ananias. The Lord Jesus appeared to him in a vision. "Ananias, you must go to the house of Judas," said the Lord. "There you must ask for Saul of Tarsus. He has been blinded, and now he is praying. He has had a vision in which a man named Ananias comes to him and places his hands on him, restoring his sight."

Ananias was fearful. "But Lord, I've heard about this man. He's come here to arrest all who are believers."

Jesus answered quietly, "Ananias, go to him. I have chosen him to be my messenger both to the Jews and to the people of other nations."

Ananias nervously set out for the house of Judas. Once there, he forced himself to knock on the door. He was quickly admitted and was shown into the room where Saul was waiting.

Ananias went forward and placed his hands on Saul, as Jesus had told him to. "Saul," he said, "Jesus has sent me to you."

At that moment, it seemed as if something like fish scales fell from Saul's eyes. His face began to shine with joy.

"I can see!" he cried excitedly. "I can see!"

Weak from his three days of fasting, Saul shakily stood up. Quietly, he spoke. "I believe," he said. "And I want to be baptized."

So Saul was baptized immediately.

Saul stayed with the believers in Damascus for a while. He used as much energy in helping them as he had previously used in having them killed. He preached in the synagogues, and everyone who heard him was utterly amazed.

Saul's preaching grew so powerful that the rulers of Damascus were not able to answer his arguments. Frightened and angry, they decided Saul must be killed. They posted guards at the city gates to capture him when he tried to leave.

But Saul's friends heard of the plot and warned him.

That night a group of believers lowered Saul down in a basket through an opening in the city wall.

Saul landed safely and quickly set out toward Jerusalem.

When he arrived in Jerusalem, Saul went to find the believers there. But they were terrified of him because of the way he'd persecuted them before. They wouldn't accept that he was now a believer too.

But Barnabas trusted Saul. He took Saul to the apostles. He told them how Saul had met Jesus on the Damascus road and how Saul had been preaching about Jesus in the synagogues of Damascus.

The apostles accepted the word of Barnabas, and the believers made Saul welcome in Jerusalem.

Just as he had done in Damascus, Saul began to preach powerfully in the synagogues. He also talked with the Greek-speaking Jews, but they became angry and plotted against his life.

When the believers discovered this, they took Saul to Caesarea. Then they sent him to Tarsus, where he would be safe.

For a while, the persecution of the churches throughout Judea, Galilee, and Samaria stopped. Through the fear of the Lord and with the comfort of the Holy Spirit, the churches grew in number.

Meanwhile, Peter traveled around the countryside, preaching about Jesus and healing the sick.

Peter Meets Cornelius

It was almost midday, and Peter had gone up to pray on the flat roof of Simon the tanner's house.

He grew very hungry. While he was waiting for a meal to be prepared, he had a vision about food.

Peter saw something that looked like a large sheet. It was being lowered down to the earth by its four corners. In the sheet were all kinds of creatures: animals, birds, and reptiles. And a voice said, "Get up, Peter. Kill and eat!"

Peter was very hungry. But according to the Law of Moses, these animals were unclean. They were not to be eaten by the Jews. Peter answered, "Oh no, Lord! I've never broken the law by eating anything which is common or unclean."

The voice spoke again. "You must not call unclean that which God has cleansed."

This happened three times. Then the sheet rose again into the sky.

Peter wondered what the vision meant. Was it only about food?

As he thought, he heard a loud knocking on the door of the house. Then the Holy Spirit spoke to Peter. "Do you hear those men? They are looking for you. I have sent them to you. Go with them."

The men had come from Caesarea with a message from Cornelius, a Roman centurion. Peter accompanied them back to Caesarea.

At last they arrived at Cornelius's house. As Peter went into the house, he began to understand the meaning of his vision. Jews had always been forbidden to visit anyone of a different nationality because foreigners were thought to be ritually unclean. They didn't keep the Jewish religious laws. But now Peter realized that no one made by God could be called "unclean."

"I realize now that God's kingdom is not just for Jews. Anyone, of any nation, who believes in God and obeys his word is acceptable to him," Peter said.

Then Peter told Cornelius and all of his friends and relatives about Jesus. As he spoke, the Holy Spirit came down on everyone who was listening, and they all began to praise God in many different languages, or tongues.

When Peter went back to Jerusalem, the believers there said, "How could you stay in the house of Gentiles?"

So Peter told them about his vision. He said, "God gave these people the Holy Spirit, just as he gave the Holy Spirit to us. How could I possibly stand against God?"

Then the believers understood and praised God. But the time of peace for them was ending.

ACTS 12:1–24

Peter in Prison

King Herod was beginning to persecute the believers again. He
arrested John's brother James and had him killed by the sword.

Peter was also thrown into prison. Herod intended to have him
killed as soon as the Festival of the Passover ended.

The believers in Jerusalem were greatly upset. They began to pray
day and night. They pleaded with God to spare Peter.

On the night before his trial, Peter was asleep in prison. He was
chained hand and foot, and the door was locked. Two soldiers were in
the cell with him to guard him. More soldiers stood outside guarding
the iron gate. Surely escape was impossible.

Then suddenly an angel woke Peter. His chains fell off with a loud
clatter, but the guards did not move. They seemed to be fast asleep.

Amazed, Peter quickly scrambled to his feet.

The angel silently opened the cell door. Peter went with him.
They passed the sleeping guards and came to the huge iron gate. To
Peter's utter amazement, the gate swung open by itself, and they
passed through into the night.

As they walked along, the angel suddenly left Peter.

Peter looked around. He really was out of prison! Peter then
hurried along the road to the house of Mary, John Mark's mother.

Inside the house, the believers were praying desperately for Peter.
Suddenly they heard a loud knocking at the outer door.

A young woman named Rhoda went to answer it.

Guessing that whoever answered the door would be alarmed,
Peter called out, "It's me, Peter!"

Peter! Rhoda was overjoyed. Not stopping to open the door, she
ran straight back to tell the other believers.

Although they had been praying for this very thing, they didn't
believe her. At last the believers went together to open the door, and
they saw him.

They took Peter inside and listened eagerly as he told them what had happened. "Tell James and the other believers about this," said Peter. Then he quietly left.

In the morning there was a great commotion at the prison. None of the guards could explain how Peter had completely disappeared.

Herod was furious. He commanded that all of the guards be executed.

Then Herod left Judea and went to Caesarea. There he made a speech to the people. Hoping to gain favor with Herod, the people shouted, "Surely he speaks not as a man, but as a god!"

Herod listened proudly, doing nothing to stop them or to give honor to the true God. An angel struck Herod down, and he died.

But the good news of the Gospel continued to spread.

Saul's First Journey

When the believers scattered after the killing of Stephen, some of them went to Antioch. Barnabas was among the believers in Antioch, and he invited Saul to come to Antioch to help with the new church. Saul came. And it was at Antioch that the believers were first called Christians, followers of Jesus Christ.

But God wanted Saul and Barnabas to take the good news to other places. So they left Antioch. John Mark, a young cousin of Barnabas, went with them as a helper.

The three men came to Pamphylia. There John left the group and went home. But Saul, now known as Paul, traveled on with Barnabas.

They reached another Antioch, this one in Pisidia. The Jews there asked Paul to preach in their synagogue. Gentiles as well as Jews came to listen to Paul's powerful sermons.

But the Jews didn't want to share the good news about Jesus with the Gentiles. They made trouble in the town for Paul and Barnabas, so the two men left Antioch and went to Iconium.

Much the same thing happened in Iconium. They then went to visit the towns of Lystra and Derbe and the surrounding area.

After facing many challenges, they at last arrived back at Antioch, the town from which they had begun their journey.

And the two apostles stayed a long time in Antioch.

ACTS 20:7–12

The Boy Who Fell Asleep

On a warm Saturday evening in an upstairs room in Troas, Paul was speaking to the believers. He had much to say, for he was leaving the next day. When midnight came, Paul was still talking.

In the room, a boy named Eutychus had perched on a window ledge to listen. Now as Paul spoke on and on, Eutychus dozed off.

He fell out of the window, and he hit the ground with a thud, three floors below.

There was a great commotion. Everyone rushed downstairs and outside. Eutychus lay very still on the ground.

Someone lifted up the boy. "He's dead!" they said.

Gently they laid him down again. Paul pressed his way to the front and threw himself on top of Eutychus and hugged him. "It's all right," he said. "Don't be afraid. He's alive."

While the boy was attended to, Paul and most of the others went back upstairs. There they broke bread together, and Paul continued talking until daybreak. Then Paul set off once more on his journeys.

After the meeting ended, Eutychus was brought in very much alive. Everyone was amazed and comforted.

Paul in Trouble

Paul had gone to visit the Temple in Jerusalem. There he was recognized by some of the Jews who had opposed him when he had visited their cities. They cried out, "Men of Israel, help! This is the man who teaches everyone against our people and against our law. He's also brought Gentiles into this Temple, defiling this holy place!"

The accusations were not true, but a riot started. Paul was seized by a mob of people and dragged out of the Temple. The people began trying to kill Paul.

A messenger rushed to inform the Roman commander whose job it was to keep peace in the city. Gathering some of his soldiers, the commander ran quickly to the place where the crowd was. When they saw the soldiers coming, the mob stopped beating Paul.

The commander arrested Paul and ordered that he be chained. "Who is this man?" he asked. The crowd shouted accusations angrily.

Fearing a riot, the commander ordered that Paul be taken inside the barracks. "Flog him and question him. Find out the truth."

As the flogging was about to start, Paul asked the centurion standing there, "Is it lawful for you to flog a Roman citizen when nothing has been proved against him?"

The centurion thought for a moment. Then he went to the commander. "Sir, this man says he is a Roman citizen."

They both knew the danger of flogging a Roman citizen without first having a trial and finding him guilty. But the commander still wanted to find out why the Jews were accusing Paul so angrily.

So the commander ordered an assembly of the Sanhedrin and brought Paul to stand before them. But a great dissension arose between the Pharisees and the Sadducees, and the commander had Paul returned to the barracks.

Paul was disappointed because he felt that he'd lost a chance to speak to the Jewish leaders. But God spoke to him in a vision. "Take heart, Paul! You have witnessed for me in Jerusalem. Now you will witness for mc in Rome."

That night, to save Paul from yet another attempt on his life, the commander sent him under a large guard to Caesarea. Felix, the governor there, could arrange the trial.

Felix had Paul imprisoned in Herod's palace until a new trial could be arranged. Then once more Paul stood before the Sanhedrin. This time he was allowed to speak. But Felix made no judgment.

So Paul was imprisoned again. After two years Felix was transferred, but he left Paul in prison to please the Jews.

Festus, the new governor, treated Paul with kindness. He asked Paul if he would like to go back to Jerusalem for a retrial.

"No," said Paul. "I want to be tried by Caesar in a Roman court."

Festus agreed to his request.

Paul and some other prisoners were placed on a ship bound for Italy.

The ship's passage had been delayed by bad weather. Now as it lay at anchor in Crete, Paul warned the centurion in charge of the danger of sailing on. But the centurion decided to set sail, hoping they could get as far as Phoenix before winter set in.

At first there was a fair wind. But soon a fierce storm came up, and the ship was driven helplessly before it. The situation became desperate.

The crew and the prisoners gave up all hope of being saved. Then Paul stood up to address them. "Take heart! For an angel of my God came to me this night and said, 'Don't be afraid, Paul! You will stand trial in front of Caesar. God will save the lives of everyone who sails with you in this ship.' I trust that it will happen exactly as God has said. But be warned, we will run aground on an island."

Sure enough, on the fourteenth night of the voyage, the sailors could tell that the ship was nearing land. They dropped four anchors, hoping to hold the ship off the rocks.

When daylight came, they saw they were near a sandy bay. They tried to beach the ship there, but it ran aground. Huge waves began to break the ship apart. "Kill the prisoners before they escape!" shouted the soldiers.

"No," responded the centurion. "Jump overboard, all of you. Swim or grab a plank. Get yourselves to land somehow."

They obeyed his order, and everyone reached the shore in safety.

Publius, the chief official of the island, provided food and shelter for the shipwrecked men. When Paul learned that Publius's father was sick, Paul went to him and healed him. Afterward many sick people came to Paul for healing.

It was three months before the shipwrecked men set sail again in a different ship. But finally Paul arrived at his destination—the city of Rome.

In Rome, Paul was allowed to rent a private home with only one soldier to guard him. He was under house arrest and could not leave, so the people came to him. Paul continued to preach fearlessly.

But in A.D. 64, there was a huge fire in Rome. The Emperor Nero blamed the Jews for the fire, and a relentless persecution of Jews and Christians began.

During that time, many of the Christians who refused to give up their faith were killed. Paul is believed to be one of those put to death at that time.

But through his words, Paul continued to influence the church. While imprisoned, he had spent much of his time writing letters to new Christians. Many of his letters were saved and read over and over again.

These letters are in the Bible, along with letters from James, Peter, John, and Jude. They are full of encouragement, instruction, and wisdom; and they are still treasured by Christians today.

John's Vision

God sent John a vision of the future.

John wrote, "After the judgment, I saw a new heaven and a new earth. I heard a voice out of heaven saying, 'Behold! God is with men, and he will dwell with them. God shall wipe away all tears from their eyes; and there shall be no more death, nor sorrow, nor crying; there shall be no more pain, for these things have passed away.'

"The holy city shall be very beautiful, for the glory of God shall be its light. Then Jesus said, 'Behold! I am coming soon!' The grace of our Lord Jesus Christ be with you all."